***SHE NEEDS:* BLUE HAIR, A BELLY BUTTON RING, A CELL PHONE, A THREE A.M. CURFEW, AND A WARDROBE LIKE HER FAVORITE ROCK STAR'S.**

YOU NEED: HELP!!!

Packed full of hands-on tips, tricks, and practical advice from other mothers in the trenches with their daughters' adolescence, this invaluable guide explains why it is vital to:

- Accept that your daughter is a distinct person—not a little version of you
- Not be afraid to be hated, because you will be—for at least an hour
- Learn how to answer the inevitable question: "But Mom, don't you trust me?"
- Understand that just because you breastfed her doesn't mean you're bosom buddies
- Be true to yourself, and do not change your looks, your opinions, and your lifestyle to suit you daughter's ever-changing whims
- Realize that it's a normal phase when she tells you…

WHEN WE'RE IN PUBLIC, PRETEND YOU DON'T KNOW ME

When We're in Public, Pretend You Don't Know Me

Surviving Your Daughter's Adolescence So You Don't Look Like an Idiot and She Still Talks to You

SUSAN BOROWITZ

WARNER BOOKS

An AOL Time Warner Company

Warner Books, Inc., 1271 Avenue of the Americas, New York, NY 10020
Visit our Web site at www.twbookmark.com

 An AOL Time Warner Company

Printed in the United States of America

First Printing: April 2003
10 9 8 7 6 5 4 3

Library of Congress Cataloging-in-Publication Data

Borowitz, Susan.
    When we're in public, pretend you don't know me : surviving your daughter's adolescence so you don't look like an idiot and she still talks to you / Susan Borowitz.
        p. cm.
    Includes index.
    ISBN 0-446-67951-8
    1. Teenage girls--United States. 2. Mothers and daughters--United States. 3. Adolescence. I. Title.

HQ78 .B635 2003
306.874'3--dc21

                                                                    2002193357

Text design by Meryl Sussman Levavi/Digitext
Cover design by Brigid Pearson
Cover illustration by Mary Lynn Blasutta

To Alexandra, the wonderful reason
why I'm both a mom and uncool.

and

To Max, my sweet pumpkin,
who some day will be my next teen.

I love you both, forever and always,
and there's nothing you can do about it.

And finally
To Mom—thanks.

Acknowledgments

First and foremost, I'd like to thank Dr. Ava L. Siegler, who in lending her wisdom and expertise to this project has provided invaluable words of guidance and support to many moms of teens, especially me. Also, thanks go to Dr. David Eger for steering me toward Dr. Siegler—I am forever indebted; my agents Coleen O'Shea, Marilyn Allen, and Bob Diforio for believing in me and this book; all my Uncool Moms, especially L. and N., who gave me many stories, and G., who gave me her wonderful words and equally wonderful support; Nora Krug, the editor at the *New York Times* who got the whole Uncool ball rolling, and Candy Lee, who knew exactly what to do with that ball; Dr. John J. Stine for everything; and very special thanks to my editor, Beth de Guzman, who with the patience of Job supported me through thick and thin. As for my at-home support group, thanks go to my husband, Andy Borowitz, for all his encouragement and the cooking and single fathering he had to do while I was stuck in front of a computer; to Polly Hunt, nanny extraordinaire, master tea-maker, occasional typist, chauffeur, general helpmate, and valued friend; and especially to my children, Alexandra and Max, who understood the inherent contradiction of me working like crazy and sometimes being a lousy mom to write a book about being a good mom.

Contents

When We're in Public, Pretend You Don't Know Me

1. The Best of Times, the Worst of Times

You know, Mom, you're hardly a perfect mother.
—my daughter, 12

In the Beginning

It all starts when we read our baby daughters the childhood classic, *The Runaway Bunny.* The fantasy of that ubiquitous mommy, who transforms into everything from a gardener to a weather condition just so she can always be with her little bunny, is so seductive and heartwarming that we quickly adopt as our own dream the notion of being forever close to our little girls. There's only one problem: They grow up. There comes a time in your daughter's life when hanging out with Mom is as appealing to her as discussing gastric problems with your own elderly mother is to you.

The question is: "When *is* that time?" Just a good look around any shopping mall with a Gap, and you will come to a disturbing conclusion. Not only do few women know the answer to that question, an appallingly small number even know that the question exists.

This book not only poses the question, but also attempts to give the answer, as well as describing the pitfalls that emerge when a woman tries to be her daughter's "best bud." The worst of these is the middle-aged compulsion to become as hip or cool as a teen at a time when it is most important for us to be uncool. In fact, it is our responsibility to be uncool in the eyes of our daughters, whose fledgling identities do not need the threat of a premenopausal mother in a belly shirt lip-synching Britney Spears.

"The two worst times in a woman's life are when she is thirteen and when her daughter is thirteen" is a maxim well known in psychology circles (to be completely accurate, add ages nine, ten, eleven, twelve, fourteen, fifteen . . . you get the point). During those years of being a mother of an adolescent—the bewilderness years—women are often at a loss as to how to handle their kids, as well as how they should handle themselves vis-à-vis their kids.

Ignorance Is Bliss

If anyone cornered the bright-eyed young women who dream of the day when a sweet little soul calls them Mommy and told them the realities of parenting a teenager, the species would abruptly come to an end.

None of us went into this with our eyes open. We were intoxicated by the sweet smell of an infant's head, as well as inundated with all the nuts and bolts of baby-rearing, which, although difficult and time-consuming, was still a task we knew we could master. After all, we hear of very few cases in which babies need to go to a doctor simply because of a loving parent's sheer lack of diapering technique; however, psychiatrists' couches are filled with people whose loving parents just screwed up during their children's adolescence because they subconsciously didn't want them to grow up and leave them.

Feeding her, changing her, burping her, even pacing the floor to calm her colicky tummy is, well, child's play compared to sending her to sleep-away camp, letting her go on her first date, dealing with the subsequent breakup, and especially pacing the floor after handing her the keys to the car. The challenges of teen-rearing are so much more exhausting and enervating than anyone ever told you they would be. Or maybe they did tell you, and you just weren't listening because you had your nose pressed onto your baby's head.

How do we manage to survive the anxieties, the heartache, the worry, and the exasperation? Well, I've repeatedly asked my husband to knock me out with a blunt, heavy object and then wake me when it's all over, but he refuses. And I've surfed the Internet trying to find a cost-effective portable Percodan drip, but I've come up empty there too. So I guess, like all of us, I'm stuck living it.

She's Right

The comment that opens this chapter ("You know, Mom, you're hardly a perfect mother") was hurled at me when I told my daughter that I was writing this book. Beyond being an example of the continual job assessment she considers her duty to perform, first and foremost it expresses the truth. I'm not. But none of us are. We're learning as we're going, and we're going to goof.

It's easy to think you're the only one goofing if you're parenting in a vacuum, so it is extremely important to get together and talk (and talk honestly—don't take it as an opportunity to brag) to other women who are going through the same daily crises as you are. It's nice to know that your daughter isn't the only one who wants to dye her hair a color found only on exotic butterflies, and it's comforting to find out that your kid isn't the only one who seems to have paranoid fantasies about the popular kids, and even more comforting to find out that they're neither paranoid nor fantasies.

Sharing the troubles that she is having with her teen helps Shelley N.* deal with the situation, which sometimes can be pretty harrowing. "I am very open with people. There are a few women where I work who also have teenagers, and I tell them everything, and it's interesting because the minute you open up, you hear all the things that are going on with their kids. And you know what? Nobody's kids are perfect and easy."

This book is a way of discussing this stage of life through my experiences, those of the many women I talked to, and the insightful comments of our "resident" psychologist, Dr. Ava L. Siegler (a leading expert in the field of adolescent and family issues). Think of us as your friends whom you can talk to about all your teenager woes. Hopefully we can help you avoid the traps that lie in wait for those moms our age who, like all of us, haven't much of a clue as to how to handle this thing called a teenage girl.

---

* All names and any identifiable information have been changed so that no daughter gets embarrassed or furious at her mom.

2. Three Types of Moms

I'll tell you three types of moms—
Annoying, Aggravating, and Pesky.
—*my daughter, 13*

Who Will You Be?

Not long ago I witnessed a stressful moment for a young mother who seemed almost desperate when faced with the horrific reality of her adorable four-year-old someday growing up.

She was in a bookstore cheerfully buying a stack of books to read to her daughter—obviously a favorite activity for both of them. When she mentioned to the cashier that they were both excited about starting the Winnie-the-Pooh stories, the cashier, an older mom, praised her and shared her pleasant experiences of reading to her own daughter when she was a cherub: "I read to her until she was nine," Cashier Mom said, ruefully adding, "and then she thought she was too cool for it."

I could see fear gripping Pooh Mom as her face turned ashen. "I am *really* not looking forward to that time, when she gets too cool for me and won't let me hug or kiss her," she said. This woman, I thought, who cherishes the special time she spends with her little girl so much, what course will she choose when she does become—and she will in fact become—uncool in her daughter's eyes?

Three Types of Moms

Clueless Mom

We who have cherubs—all of us—must make a choice when our babies first roll their eyes at us in disgust. Some women choose to ignore the fact that teenage attitude and separation are both part of a necessary stage of life. I call them the Clueless Moms. They deal with the problem of their daughters growing up by forcing the girls to share their own view of the world— that they have a loving relationship and that nothing as irritating as teen rebellion is going to shake it. Mom will always be Mom; Daughter will always be her little girl. They give their kids zero control over their own lives and are usually overprotective.

Best Bud Mom

Other women manage the threat of losing such a warm and chummy relationship by continuing the warm and chummy relationship into the teen years. These are the Best Bud Moms, and they deal with their daughters' growing independence by forcing themselves into their adolescents' views of the world. If Daughter is going to have a new teenage life, Mom's coming along. And since they're friends, anything goes—no limits! Best Bud Moms give their kids total (and premature) control over their own lives.

Uncool Mom

An Uncool Mom recognizes that she and her daughter are two separate individuals with two distinct lives. She is warmly supportive and active in setting limits, but knows where to draw the line. Her job is to bring up her child to be a happy, healthy, and productive member of society, and she thinks the best way is to let her grow into the role of adult—to take control of her life bit by bit—which means that Mom has a lot of painful letting go to do.

To help me navigate this rough terrain, I use one indispensable tool: remembering my own adolescence and how

What Kind of Mom Are You?

	Clueless Mom	Uncool Mom	Best Bud
You wear:	half of a mother/daughter matching Laura Ashley set	Gap jeans and shirt	an ensemble from the Christine Aguilera collection
You let your daughter:	out of her room for school	go	wear a Wonderbra to the fourth grade picnic
On your daughter's first date, you:	wish her a happy fortieth birthday and good luck	invite the boy in to meet him	hope her boyfriend thinks you're a hottie
Your teen is having a party. You:	make sure there are enough seats for Musical Chairs	make sure you're going to be home	make sure they've got enough beer
Your daughter has gained a few extra pounds. You:	pinch her chubby cheeks and call her "Chubby Cheeks" in public	make her cut down on french fries and start exercising	tell her you're both fat and share your diet pills with her
You think your teen daughter is:	too young for bras, boys, or rebellion	ruled by her hormones	your BFF and gossip pal

important and difficult those years were to me, the teen, as well as to my own mother.

A Declaration of Independence

I recall one of my earliest attempts at teen rebellion. My mother, to whom I had been extremely close as a young child, was annoying me in a way that only mothers can annoy their adolescent girls: She was being my mother.

Of course there were times when she would do much more active things that mortified me and therefore I hated, such as humming while washing the dishes, or standing with her left knee cocked, forcing her left foot en pointe behind her, or sometimes making a high-pitched whistle when she breathed through her nostrils—all of it was torture. But this was worse: She was asking me about my day at school.

I was tired of being the dependent little kid who came home to Mommy after school. I really wanted to spread my thirteen-year-old wings and show her I didn't need her any more and that it was high time she got off my back. How dare she ask me about my day? Who did she think I was—her child? It suddenly struck me that this was as good a time as any to be a smart-mouth.

"Face it, Mom. You're obsolete," I said.

I had recently learned the word from a series of kitchen counter-top commercials. I forget the actual product, but whatever it was, "it made Formica obsolete." Like any good seventh-grader, I looked up the word. And like any good student, I knew that I just had to use it three times and it would be mine. One down; two to go.

Bull's-eye!

Mom didn't see it coming. She thought we were having fun just as we always had—me with my afternoon snack, her with her questions that I now viewed as interrogation. Fun, and then shock. "You're obsolete." It hit her smack between the eyes, and the impact seemed to bring an incipient tear. Uh-oh. Did I do that?

"C'mon, Mom, I'm sorry. I didn't mean it," I called out to her as she left the room. I swore to myself that I'd never use that word again, and therefore it would never, ever be mine.

In fact, I can't hear or see the word today without being reminded of the time I tried to be tough and independent, to break free and take a shot at the impervious goliath I called Mom only to see her crumble. Was this one of those incidents that she would often refer to as another nail in her coffin?

My Turn

Now, thirty years later, it is my turn to be obsolete. It is my turn to relinquish the role of MVP in my daughter's life gradually by allowing her to grow up, break away, and ultimately depend on herself. Completely. Without me. Whether I like it or not. Motherhood is the most time-honored and effective form of planned obsolescence since the world emerged from primordial soup. VCR manufacturers can't do better.

So why do I accept becoming obsolete to my own flesh and blood? Because it's the natural course of things. Because I don't want my adult daughter screening her calls to avoid me.

Raise 'Em, and Release 'Em

The job of mothers is to raise the next generation and then let them go—a new crop of competent adults. But there is one type of mother who fails to do this: the one who thinks that her nose will be welcome in every aspect of her daughter's life no matter how old her baby gets, the overattached mommy who resists any attempt her daughter makes to separate from her. She may think she does it all out of love, but she is breaking a lot of laws that Nature had intended every childbearing female to uphold. Can you imagine a mother beaver visiting her grown daughter's dam and rearranging the sticks without asking?

We all know about these meddlesome biddies whose adult daughters have at some point fervently wished that Mom could somehow procure a life. So why on Earth would so many young mothers of today blithely wander down the path that will eventually lead to becoming such a person? Answer: so that no one can ever tell them that they are obsolete, because that kind of obsolescence—maternal obsolescence— can really hurt.

The Wonder of Motherhood

From the moment she is born, you are the most important person in your daughter's life, which is absolutely intoxicating. With each change of diaper, with each infant smile (don't believe that "gas" mumbo jumbo—it's a smile and it's only for you), and with each cuddle after a bad dream, accompanied by her tears wiped on your neck, you fall deeper and deeper into the black hole of mommy-ness until, by the time preschool strikes, you're completely hooked.

Sometimes, especially when everything else went wrong

that day, she could still thrill you by squeaking and flailing her chubby little arms in the direction of the maternal lap the minute your eyes met. And then there are all the wonderful and magical moments you shared with your little angel as she grew—scaring away monsters from her room, enjoying tea parties, receiving handmade birthday gifts that you couldn't quite identify—the list goes on forever. So when baby hits adolescence and it's time to start letting go, well, let's just say that Betty Ford probably should have opened up a clinic for this kind of dependency too.

But let go we must, with all the attendant pain. Teenage daughters don't adore their mothers anymore, and the only time they squeak and flail their arms at you is when you've just grounded them. And then you remember the way it used to be, and it breaks your heart. It breaks your heart to go from being the only one she wants to being the only one she wants to strangle.

Give Me Relevance or Give Me Death

However, none of this pain justifies acting like an idiot. The specific idiots that I'm referring to belong to a large collection of women who make every effort, regardless of how damaging it may be to their daughters or how discomfiting it is for the rest of us, never to become obsolete. This group further breaks down into the two major subsets we discussed earlier: those who achieve their dubious goal by preventing their daughters from growing up at all—the Clueless Moms—and the Best Bud Moms—those who do it by becoming their daughter's best friend, or as I call it, "best bud." I gleaned this hip phrase right out of the pages of the guidebooks that no forty-something Best Bud Mom can live without: *Teen* magazine and *J-14*.

Clueless Mom

The Clueless Mom is not immediately recognizable. On the surface she seems perfect—she's got her family under control with a completely docile teenager to prove it (docile . . . for now). She artificially extends her daughter's childhood either through covert pressure ("If you never let me hug you again, it would break my heart") or drill sergeant strictness. Although she looks and seems to act like any sane person, lurking beneath that normal exterior is a woman who would be happy to continue the nightly readings of *The Berenstain Bears Say Please and Thank You* to her daughter even when she has to push her son-in-law out of bed to do it. She is either blind to and doesn't acknowledge the young popular culture that her teen so desperately wants to embrace ("Britney Spears—she's that little red-headed girl who bit you in preschool, right?") or so threatened by it that she forbids it to enter the house. Understandably, she is completely embarrassing to her daughter.

The only way to identify Mrs. Clueless is when she's with her teenage daughter, who will invariably be dressed as her favorite American Girl doll. Laura Ashley is the designer of choice, which gets problematic when all that smocking begins to emphasize the girl's growing bustline. In this mom's mind it's okay to keep her daughter a little girl and then at eighteen send her off to a fine university with her innocence intact and an armload of kilts. I remember those kinds of girl from my college days. By mid-September freshman year, they realized that they were something referred to as a "woman," went a little wild, and well, the rest is history—history probably carved into the bathroom stall in the men's dormitories.

Possible Causes

What makes a Clueless Mom so clueless? Perhaps when her little girl was actually *little*, she took that "Mommy always comes back" mantra a bit too seriously. It made sense to chant that to our children when they were very young and still desperately needed us, but as they get older, it's more important for them to know that they can stand on their own two feet. When they're adults, the phrase "Mommy always comes back" sounds like an advertisement for *Psycho III*.

I've got news for Clueless Mom: There's going to come a time when Mommy doesn't come back. Ever. Maybe it is the inevitability of the years being ripped off the calendar that propels many women into such regrettable behavior. Perhaps aging is so freaky to them that subconsciously they think that if they can make sure their daughters never grow up, they will never get old.

Best Bud Mom

Clueless Moms are more a problem for their kids than they are to the rest of us moms, since rarely do children come home from school complaining, "Megan isn't allowed to watch TV! How come I am?!" No, for me, the women who make life difficult are the Best Bud Moms. These are the moms who look and act "cool," the moms who get matching eighty-dollar haircuts for themselves and their barely-out-of-single-digits-aged daughters (What's good for the goose is good for the gosling), the moms who are not terribly familiar with the word no, the moms who make perfectly reasonable limits and rules seem like an eighteen-year stint at Sing-Sing.

Whereas Clueless deals with the inexorable passage of

time by trying to freeze it, thereby cryogenically preserving her daughter in a perpetual state of childhood, Best Bud's own little time warp involves entering the teenage years with her daughter (sort of a second adolescence prelude to the geriatric second childhood). She feels that they have been so close during her child's early years that continuing into the teen years with a friendship just makes sense. If you find yourself leaning in that direction, remind yourself: Just because you nursed her doesn't mean you're bosom buddies.

All mothers love doing things with and being with their little girls, but there comes a time when the girls are going to want to move on and do a lot of the fun stuff with their peers. This is the start of the separation process, and the healthiest thing you can do is let them go. Remember: Separation is not a team sport, and if you find yourself saying, "Sweetie, I know you need to separate, and I'm thrilled—it'll be something we can do together!" then it's time to reevaluate your approach.

What's Wrong with Being Close?

Nothing. The Best Bud's wish to be close to her daughter may originate from more than a desire to continue the warmth of a cozy relationship. It's possible that this urge to be so chummy may stem from her desire to know everything that is going on in her child's life so that she can make sure her kid doesn't get into destructive behaviors such as drinking or taking drugs—a goal that is both understandable and admirable.

The problem arises when a mother confuses having a friend or peer (i.e., nonauthority) relationship with having a close or good relationship with her daughter. You can have a loving relationship with your child without having to be her friend.

Similarly, you can have a good relationship with her while still giving her the chance to break away from you, all the while exercising responsible authority over her. But take note: A "good" relationship does not always mean (and with teenagers it rarely means) an idyllic relationship.

Even so, the benevolent motive of a parent wanting to be close to keep her child out of trouble doesn't account for why so many Best Bud Moms prematurely grant their kids privileges that they aren't ready to handle (like going to the mall by themselves at age nine and lax or nonexistent curfews), thus exposing them to opportunities to get involved in the destructive behaviors that most of us want our kids to avoid. Believe it or not, I've even heard stories of moms who smoke pot with their high school–aged children. I guess the family who tokes together, chokes together.

Friends?

Let's look at the reality of being best friends with someone who is at least a quarter century younger than you. If you consider what women actually do with their best friends, the notion seems either really weird or just bogus. Is there any woman (who should not be under constant surveillance by the Child Welfare Agency) who actually treats her daughter as she does her best friends—discussing her marital problems, sharing sexual or financial concerns, using raw language about things that are plaguing her, such as her own overbearing, nutty mother? I think it's safe to assume that people need best friends who are not dependent on them for an ethical, stable, or sane upbringing. Let your children be your children; find your friends at the PTA. Which brings up another point—are these women so pathetic and unpopular that they have to breed to get a best friend? Where will it all end? It certainly suggests one possible frightening misuse of cloning technology.

On the daughter's side of the equation, what sort of hubris leads the Best Bud Moms into presuming that they're such groovy chickies that their daughters actually *want* them as their best buds? More important, what kid wants any friend who's in her forties? When I was a teen, one of my requirements for a best friend was that if I was ever menstrually unprepared, my friend should be able to reach into her purse and produce a tampon, not a hormone replacement pill.

The truth is, we never wanted our own mothers for best friends (for many, the feeling persists through adulthood as well), and our daughters are most likely following suit. Best friends are those you complain to *about* your mother, and believe me, no matter how wonderful a mother is, there will always be teenage complaining to do. Complaining for teenage girls is a right, a sacrament, and an involuntary compulsion that falls somewhere between shrieking when they see each other, and breathing.

"But I'm Too Young to Have a Teenager!"

If the primary goal of Best Bud Mom is to be her adolescent daughter's best friend, she achieves that questionable position by aging herself down and her daughter up to about seventeen years old. The unfortunate result is a preteen kid pushed to grow up too fast, with too many privileges and too little guidance, and a mother who makes Miss Havisham the model of living in the present. This behavior may make the mom feel that she's as young as she keeps telling herself she is, but it drags the poor unsuspecting kid down the dark chasm of her mother's ugly little midlife crisis. Should a child of such tender years (as well as the rest of the community) be subjected to her mother's crepey midsection every time the woman dons a crop-top? Now I know that whenever *I* intend to do something monstrously, cataclysmically insane, I make an extra effort not to include my daughter.

If you pick your child up at school or attend any school functions, it is impossible to avoid these crop-topped, low-rise panted matrons. In my community, they collect like silt by the doors of the school creating a sort of knockoff Prada obstruction that you must slog through to get to your child. These middle-aged women gather into their cliques wearing too-tight Capris that show off not only postgestational potbellies that the rest of us have the good sense to camouflage, but also the latest, hottest ankle bracelet, which daintily sets off broken capillaries as well as spider veins.

Abbey S. tells of the escapades of the Best Buds in her community. "There are mothers who are in their mid-forties and fifties in these little teenage outfits. It really scares me— that mom who wants to fit in and be like her kid. They were at the fifth grade school dance acting like teenagers. They were dancing with the hired dancers. They were up on stage as if they were saying, 'Hey, look at us! We may be older, but we are so cool—we know how to do all the dances that our kids should be doing.' And their kids were stuck in the corner. I wanted to say, 'Why are you having more fun than your kid at your kid's school dance?'"

Possible Root Causes

I believe that same fear of aging that hounds Clueless is also behind the bizarre behavior of the Best Bud Moms. With one ill-advised stroke, they think they can tackle the problem of keeping a daughter who is separating close by, as well as the problem of getting old. But when this results in, as it has in my town, a woman picking up her daughter from day camp in a bikini, neither goal is reached. It embarrasses the girl, and doesn't make the mom look young, just senile.

Are they even aware of what they are doing? They are obviously not aware of how they look. My guess is that this is not the culmination of a life dressing as if they were constantly peddling their feminine wares; they probably dressed more conservatively when they were younger (a lot of these women used to have serious careers). But these women have hit a point in their lives when they realize that Chad, the hot-looking twenty-something tennis pro at their club, is calling them "ma'am," and that requires immediate action.

In their fear of losing their sexual relevance, they desperately try to leave no stone or head unturned. Like the exotic Mexican agave plant that after thirty-five dignified years as a quiet set of leaves nears the end of its usefulness and shoots out a skyscraper of a stalk flush with a gaudy spectacle of yellow blossoms, the Best Bud Mom approaches the perimenopausal years encased in hot pants and tube tops in one last burst of fecundity before the game is over. Too bad the daughter tends to be along for the ride.

And Now for an Opposing View

There will always be those mothers determined to stay young who say, "But this is the twenty-first century! Things are different these days. I am still incredibly cool and young. I exercise. I look great for forty." First of all, looking great for forty is not necessarily the same thing as looking great. There is value in looking great at forty, just please, can we do it with a little taste and elegance, and recognize that being cool is now the sole domain of people our daughters' age? Second, when any woman takes the serious step into parenthood, she has to realize that her daughter's emotional well-being must always supercede her own desire to act like a moron.

Let's say for the sake of argument that you're in great shape and you're looking better than ever. Congratulations! But you have to realize that your beauty does not give you carte blanche to embarrass or annoy your daughter by trying to look like one of her peers. My daughter tells me that even though girls want their moms to look pretty, they really want them to look like moms, not like competition.

No Is Not a Four-Letter Word

Looking like she's lost count of her birthdays two decades ago is a quirk of the Best Bud Mom that only embarrasses herself and her daughter. The damage from her "best friend" philosophy of parenting comes when, in order not to be hated by her child, she finds it impossible to say no to her. Now not being able to say no to a younger kid might result in the house looking a lot like a Toys "R" Us stockroom, but when the kid gets bigger, the things she's going to want will be a lot less innocuous.

One woman, Lynn W., told me a frightening story of a family from her hometown. The mother was so intent on having a close relationship with her kids that she allowed her thirteen-year-old daughter to have a twenty-eight-year old boyfriend during a vacation in Spain; back at home, she provided a convenient little refrigerator where her teens could keep their beer. Lynn says, "She was a really nice woman, but maybe too nice. There were absolutely no limits, and the family was a mess."

Of course, Lynn's story is an extreme example, but more subtle versions are happening daily in your own neighborhood. Mothers, who probably mean well, can't set limits for their kids. They let them dress like adults (slutty adults, that is) and behave like adults when they are as young as eight, nine, or ten because "it looks so cute." It's almost as if they think their kids have the consciousness of infants, whom you can dress up and pose like gangsters, and they'll retain none of it. Preteens and young adolescents, however, retain all of it, are influenced by all of it, and start actually playing the part, which, when they get to be full-fledged teens, is not "so cute." If limits are never set, they'll be off and running. Good luck trying to catch them.

Enter the Uncool Mom

So what about the rest of us—the moms who try to be responsible mothers, but who also try to let their daughters find themselves? We are the Uncool Moms. We set reasonable limits, but allow them the room to grow. More important, we act like mothers, like women our own ages, which is one of the best ways I think a parent can set an example and send to her child the message that she should be comfortable with who she is, that she doesn't have to succumb to the pressure to be cool—a pressure that can lead to drinking, drugs, and all that other behavior that keeps parents up at night.

"Uh-oh," you say, "I must not be Uncool because I like talking to my daughter and being close." Relax. There is nothing about being Uncool that suggests that you can't be a warm, loving, and supportive figure in your daughter's life. As a matter of fact, the Uncool Mom talks to her daughter a lot, but in a style that doesn't prohibit her from growing up and pulling away. But no matter what, a good mom is a mom who keeps the channels of communication open with her teen as much as she possibly can.

The Uncool Mom is aware of her daughter's life, but she's also aware that she should be only a part of it. She's concerned enough to know what her kid is up to, but doesn't need to know all the gossipy details. She has no proprietary interest in her child's pop culture because she has her own. She understands that her job is to be her child's mother, and she's not afraid to be an authority figure, yet she manages to do the job lovingly. And with all that, she still finds time to be obsolete.

Harder than It Looks

It sounds easy, but it isn't. In fact, when your daughter comes to one of those moments in her adolescent life that requires a decision from you, such as a teen party, it's much easier to be Clueless and just say no, forbidding any parties except those given by you. It's also much easier to be a Best Bud and just say "go" and let her do whatever she wants.

The difficult choice is being Uncool, because as an Uncool Mom, you can't fall back on knee-jerk reactions. You constantly have to be reevaluating your daughter's maturity and attitude to make sound judgments as to what she is capable of handling responsibly. A teen party? Before the Uncool Mom can give her permission, she has to talk to her kid about it, check out who the host is, find out if parents will be there, and so on, and then weigh it all to make a reasonable decision that tries to balance a parent's desire to protect with an adolescent's need to try out her wings. It's tough, tiring, and will probably annoy your daughter. But at least you'll know that either she's going to be safe attending a fun and harmless party, or she'll be safe at home, not attending a potentially dangerous party. The most important thing is to allow her to grow up and become her own person, but at a rate she can handle by herself.

Your Services Will No Longer Be Needed

So give me obsolescence. The babe-moms can go their cool little collagen-enhanced way. I stand up to the tyranny of cool. I am Uncool. I am a mother. I may make my share of mistakes, but I am trying my hardest to do the healthiest and most natural thing: to raise a happy, well-adjusted daughter, and then get mercilessly rejected. Then I will know that my mission is complete and has been successful. Motherhood is the one career position that when you do the best job possible, you are sure to be fired. I won't be getting my final pink slip for a few years yet, but when I do, I'll be ready.

3. Why It's Cool to Be Uncool

All this "uncoolness" stuff is really dorky.
—*my daughter, 13*

A Word or Two about Coolness

Coolness is our generation's obscure object of desire. From the moment of our first awareness of cool, probably sometime in grade school when we realized that nobody wanted to be Ringo when we played Beatles, it has been sort of a Holy Grail that would admit whoever found it to the heaven of Popularity. All through our early years, our social relevance depended on it, and unfortunately, unlike that other scourge of our youth, acne, most of us don't outgrow the obsession with or at least the concern about coolness.

We feel compelled to wear the right clothes, listen to the right music, drive the right car, drink the right wine, and watch the right TV shows as if our lives depended on it. Imagine being in a conversation at a party in which you're the only one who didn't like, or (horrors!) never watched, *Sex in the City*. Would you tell the truth? Unless you enjoy being contrary, probably not. Not at the risk of being thought of as "not with it" or uncool. So what exactly does it mean to be cool?

Think about the Icons of Cool, like Elvis or James Dean, guys who are to coolness what Thomas Jefferson is to democracy. What made them cool? (Elvis and Dean, not Jefferson.) Answer—they weren't trying. They didn't seem to care what anybody thought. And they certainly were not campaigning to be anyone's friend—everyone else wanted to be their friend. Now perhaps Elvis the person cared, but Elvis the icon didn't. That's what we all admired.

The Problem with Trying

When the Icons of Cool appear to care what people think and pander to the public, they quickly become Icons of Room Temperature. How else did Elvis morph from the King of Cool with the wayward shock of hair and insouciant smirk to the bloated joke in a spangled jumpsuit playing Vegas almost as if he were an Elvis impersonator?

A later, but no less compelling, example is Rod Stewart: very cool when he started out, but cringingly embarrassing when he tried to keep up with disco. When you get to the point when you have to ask, "Do you think I'm sexy?" I think you know what the answer is.

Of course James Dean remains an Icon of Cool. He took care of that by dying at the height of his coolness powers. However effective, this is not an attractive option for the rest of us.

Mission Impossible

The point of this is not to give you pointers on how to be cool. It is, however, an illustration of an important fact about cool-ness: It cannot be achieved through trying. Coolness is a form of cultural grace that descends upon those chosen few, and not us. You can't aspire to coolness; you can't contrive to attain it. In fact, once you try to be cool, you are caring what people think and that makes you, ipso facto, uncool.

There you have it: Coolness—it's an impossible goal and an elusive dream. Those who pursue it not only never reach it, but also look a lot goofier than if they had never tried. The next time you have even a whisper of a thought that you can be cool if only you tried, just remember Warren Beatty rapping in *Bullworth*.

Wait a Minute . . .

Now you may be thinking, "If we're not supposed to care what people think, then why should we care about looking 'goofy'?" Not looking cool is one thing. Looking like a delusional fool is another. A good test is this: If you saw behavior from someone else (say, your own mother when you were a teen) that would make you flinch and either feel sorry for her or impel you to shield the eyes of nearby young children, then it is behavior that should be avoided.

So, since trying to be cool is at best a waste of time and at worst a mortifying fool's errand, the only alternative is not to care about it. Isn't it time to throw off the onerous yoke of Cool? Don't we deserve to be able to do what we like and feel confident in what we like without worrying about our image? At the risk of quoting Lambchop, Barney, or some other piece of felt—be yourself. Do what pleases you, not some fantasy panel of public opinion experts or some imaginary bouncers at the nightclub of life.

Doing what you like will not only feel good, but it will also send a powerful message to your kids that it's okay to stand up to peer pressure and what the crowd thinks, which in this day of deadly drugs and AIDS is more important than ever. It's a lot easier to tell your kids to "just say no" and to be true to themselves when they see that Mom is happy being herself and does not try to curry anyone's favor but her own.

After several months of being cool-free, you may find that you feel somewhat liberated. Trying to be cool requires an inordinate amount of time and energy to keep up with general trends as well as what your particular coolness role models are doing, wearing, eating, and driving. Once you purge yourself of the need to be cool, think of all the junk you don't need to fill your head with, especially during this period in our lives when less and less is fitting into our heads.

Just Cool It, or Rather, Uncool It

So what does all this analysis of coolness have to do with being uncool? Simple. If you're trying to be closer to your daughter by acting like her friend, adopting her style, and shar-

---

Useful Information to Put in Your Head Instead of Coolness Clutter

- Where your kids are
- Where your glasses are
- That you need more toothpaste
- What day it is
- Everything in this book

ing her teen culture, what you are really doing is trying to be cool in her eyes. You, who like it or not are supposed to be the authority figure, are pandering to your own kid. (Only the few closet fascists among us really relish being the authority figure for our kids, but let's face it—it's one of those unfortunate requirements that come with the job, like attending grade school squeaky-clarinet orchestra performances.) Nothing puts you in a position of subordination like pandering. And in the delicate teen and adolescent years, it is essential for a child to feel that someone else (preferably a grown-up) is in charge and keeping everything together. They may chafe at your relentless authority, but they also need it. The chafing is part of the necessary process by which they grow up and become their own person so that they can inflict relentless authority on their own kids.

Meredith L., the mother of a grown daughter, said to me, "If I had it to do over again, I would be even Uncooler than I was. Especially now that kids are bombarded constantly with messages urging them to expand their appetites and go crazy and rush along with the crowd. It is very important to have someone standing in the doorway, arms crossed, saying no and meaning it. I think it gives a kid a sense of security, even if they kick against it—at least they have something to kick against."

Being your child's friend certainly makes it harder to lay down the law when it's needed. Do your daughter's school friends have a serious talk with her when she brings home a C in English? Unless things have changed dramatically from when I was a youngster, friends don't usually ground friends. The truth is, we're not made to be our adolescents' friends. If we were supposed to make friends by giving birth to them, God wouldn't have created garden clubs.

Finally, when you try to be cool in your child's eyes, you are not only undermining your authority by seeking her approval, you're *trying* to be cool. And as we've seen, that means you'll never actually be cool.

So what's the point of trying to be your daughter's hip friend? Just sit back, brace yourself, and be a mom. An Uncool Mom.

4. Separation

Shouldn't I be hating you by now?
—*my daughter, 12*

A Love/Hate Relationship

In the middle of having fun with my daughter when she was twelve and a half, she said, "Shouldn't I be hating you by now?" Trying my best to sound like Diana Ross, I answered, "You can't hurry hate." But what was actually going on in my mind was surprise. Surprise, first of all that she didn't already hate me, and second that she would be so willing to show me any vulnerability. She essentially was saying to me, "I love you and I'm having fun, and I really don't want it to change." And that, along with the opposite desire (and compulsion) to stop having fun with, break free from, and hate your parents, sums up the poignancy of this time of a young person's life: adolescence.

It also sums up the unremitting roller coaster ride that nauseates both mother and daughter (not to mention other family members) and can last as long as two presidential terms. The ups and downs, twists and turns we have to endure right along with her when at one moment she needs you desperately and the next moment she wants you out of her face just as desperately can induce a migraine. It can make a mother feel as if her darling daughter has just disappeared and she is now living with Dr. Jekyll and Mr. Hyde, or more accurately, Mr. Hyde on a good day and Mr. Hyde on a bad day.

What's It All About?

The whiplash experience that characterizes these years can be attributed not only to Nature's hormone titration experiment with teens, but also to the developmental stage called separation. Separation is the process by which a child experiences herself as a separate individual who can function autonomously, without the help of parents. For most people this starts in toddlerhood and culminates in adolescence, after years of gradually becoming more and more self-sufficient, both physically and emotionally. The teen years are so tough because that is when the complete break from the safety and comfort of Mommy and Daddy occurs. For some kids, the separation process is subtle; for others, it's more obvious; and for some kids, their separation seems as cataclysmic as the prehistoric separation of the continents, although affecting weather patterns a bit less.

Many psychologists will tell you that separation is not only normal, but also necessary for a person to develop into a well-adjusted, self-determined, and fully realized adult. In my book that spells "pretty happy." True, it can't make everything in a person's life go right, but it goes a long way in making her happy with *herself.* And when she's happy with herself, she's less likely to have an identity crisis and go about doing a bunch of regrettable things (having destructive romantic relationships, drinking too much, making empty career choices, etc.) to try to make herself complete.

Don't Put Off 'til Tomorrow . . .

The final process of separation should take place during the teenage years, not when your kid is thirty and still living in her old bedroom (you know the room I mean, the room you intend to convert someday into a media room or in-home gym, or rent out to a more grateful and paying tenant). The problem is that our society sees teen rebellion not as a necessary stage of life, but as a nasty period that is best avoided. What's more, we want to have a very close relationship with our children from their cradle to our grave. Unfortunately, this sometimes results in parents hindering the separation process, thereby retarding their children's ability to become independent adults.

We would have no problem with this concept if we were animals. Animals understand that the survival of their species is dependent on their offspring hightailing it out of their cozy little nests and going out on their own to make the next generation of babies. There aren't too many grizzly bears who crash at their mother's den, overhibernate, and refuse to get up and snag their own salmon because they're not sure what they want to do with their lives. If that were the case, the mother would attack them. And if the slacker kid happened to be a Komodo dragon or Tasmanian devil, they'd be Mama's lunch—literally.

Let Them Go Now

Of course, we're not animals, and humans don't have to worry too much about keeping their population up since we're already crowding out every other species on Earth. But the point is that Nature intended the human child to grow up and leave during the teen years, so it's foolish to fight it. (Our difficult task is keeping them from accidentally killing themselves and making sure they're responsible enough for that big break from us at age eighteen.) If they don't separate when they're teens, they may have to do it (often with the help of a therapist) when they're adults. And it's significantly harder to reject much older parents who are actually vulnerable, frail, and possibly close to death. Let them rail against you, hate you, and be miserable to you now while you are still young enough and powerful enough to take the blows.

Besides, who in her right mind wants a forty-year-old child who still depends on her so much that she calls in the middle of the night because she can't decide what color to paint her bathroom?

It's Still Bad

But does knowing any of this make it easier when your daughter turns twelve or thirteen and goes haywire? Yes and no. Yes because, at least for me, it makes it easier to put the teenage years into perspective as just another phase (although a more treacherous one considering all the trouble a teen can get into), and no because it doesn't keep the pain of the separation from hurting any less—for either of us.

So we're forced to play an emotional version of the playground game Crack the Whip with our mercurial, hormone-soaked daughters thrashing about with us at the end of the whip, holding on for dear life, our spirits getting bruised every time they change direction and we hit the wall. They want you; they don't want you. They need you; they don't need you. No one can possibly understand the true meaning of the word *dizzy* until they experience a daughter in the throes of adolescence.

From Playground Swings to Mood Swings

Shelley N. noticed that when her daughter Paige hit about thirteen, she became extremely moody and would just freak out about little things. "Once she found a spider in the bathroom, and she screeched for me to help her. She wanted me to put it outside, but my hair was wet and it was winter. As I went to flush it down the toilet, she got all upset, crying that the spider had a family. I thought she was joking, so I threw it in the toilet, and as I flushed it, as a joke I said in a high voice, 'Help me, help me, I'm drowning, somebody help me.' Well, that was it. She was hysterical. This kid cried for an hour, hour and a half. She said I had murdered the spider. It was so strange."

It's a very unsettling experience for both parent and child. Shelley says, "Girls are so overwhelmed by their emotions at this age. Every little thing gets blown out of proportion, and they can't function as they once did. I think they're learning how to be new people."

Like the Flowers Need the Rain

Learning how to be a new person is a monumental task. And if you think that all of the ups and downs are confusing for us mothers, just imagine what our daughters are going through. The truth is that at this time in their lives, our girls need us more than ever.

The standard wisdom that kids need their moms the most when they're of preschool age is, if you ask me, totally bone-headed. Yes, little kids should have their mommies around for all sorts of emotional and developmental reasons, but teenagers should also have their moms around, not only to keep them on the straight and narrow, but also to be available when they need them—for questions, a talk, emotional support.

Unfortunately for those of us who work or have other responsibilities, quantity time is as valuable as quality time because when something's bothering her, it may take a long time for her to figure out exactly what it is. It's possible for the working or overburdened mom to give her tortured teen quantity time, but it usually means that something else (that nice long hot bath, for instance) has got to go, or at least be put on hold until the day after she leaves for college.

A Trying and Tiring Time

If you thought constant diaper changes, 2 A.M. feedings, or playing Polly Pocket until you're blue in the face was tiring, just wait. The difference is that your time with your daughter now is not going to be quite as pleasant as it was when she was a tot. Her problems are harder to deal with now, and at this age she uses up a lot of your psychic energy.

Just watching our girls go through the social miseries of adolescence can be equally enervating and distressing for us. We can remember the pain of being ostracized by the popular girls more vividly than we can remember the pain of getting a booboo (unless you were a popular girl, in which case I hope you're being ostracized now). And we know that early childhood is a "gimme" compared to the adolescent years because the hurt and the anxieties of teenhood mimic very closely the hurt and anxieties of adulthood. It's a rough time of life, which is why they need us now.

The problem is that they don't want to need us. And when they don't want us around, they want us on call 24/7, just in case. If my daughter could, she would put me in a box and open it when she needs me, but I had better go right back in when she thinks I'm in the way. When she was younger and growing out of Barbies, we packed up all the dolls and clothes and put them in the attic. Periodically she would go through withdrawal and bring some down to play with, and then a few days later they'd go back up. At some point she finally kicked the habit, and Barbie stayed upstairs, she and her chesty friends packed away like sardines, her nylon hair getting bent, forgotten until the next generation is old enough to play with her. Sometimes I think that I am destined, as are all mothers, to share the same fate as that Barbie. Not the same waistline, just the same fate.

An Example

I recall the first time I really felt as though I was being packed away: when my husband and I drove our daughter to her second year at sleep-away camp. When I dropped her off at her bunk and it was time for me to go, I expected a hug and a meaningful smile to pass between us—a moment suspended in time. After all, six weeks is a pretty long spell to be away. The reality was that she so vastly preferred being with her peers that she spent a half-second throwing her twiggy arms around her dad and me and then sped off to the "teen canteen." I was left with a feeling of having the rug pulled out from under me, as well as this uncontrollable urge to do something I refuse to do at home—hang up her clothes. In retrospect, I suppose I was hoping that with her already gone, maybe I could have a "moment" with her rain parka.

The strangest reaction came a little later. At first I enjoyed the peace and quiet that goes hand-in-hand with the absence of an adolescent. But about three weeks in, I actually started to miss, not only her, but also her teen behavior. I know it seems that my inner desire to trade relative serenity for the cacophony of defiance, arguments, and sarcasm paints me as bit of a masochist, and maybe I am. Or maybe I'm just a mom.

The truth was that I was in the midst of a pain trade-off. Either I had to endure the misery of teenage insurrection or the heartache of realizing that my importance in her life was fading. Sometimes I wonder if the torment that we mothers experience as our children grow up and away from us is simply cosmic justice for when we yammered on incessantly about our babies to our childless friends.

The Torment

When the topic of sleep-away camp first came up, I anticipated living through the weeks she was away in a constant state of apprehension, dreading that phone call that would regretfully inform us of her death, hospitalization, or eye being put out by a bunkmate armed with a sharp elbow. But once she was gone, I was surprised to find myself not worrying about her safety one iota. I knew she would be fine.

In fact, I was enthusiastic about her having to deal with social problems all by herself, as well as having her least charming habits curbed due to peer disapproval. I was thrilled that when faced with something she didn't want to do, she couldn't bring out the anti-mom artillery, which is in such easy reach when she's with me, because at sleep-away camp THERE IS NO MOM.

And that, in a nutshell, was the problem. For the first

time I got the distinct impression that she was beginning to really break free of me and become independent. It was a bittersweet realization because while I was pleased that she was growing up and intellectually comfortable with her starting the teen phase of the separation process, I couldn't fully anticipate how sad and empty I would feel. The more adjusted she gets to life without me, the less important I become in her life. And I'd be lying if I said it doesn't hurt.

It's Supposed to Hurt

It's an instinctive response to try to avoid pain, but this is one pain you have to face head-on. You can't protect yourself from the pain, and unfortunately, no amount of reading or talking to mothers who are going through it can truly prepare you for how it will feel when it happens. Sound familiar? The whole process is akin to another necessarily painful time: childbirth. Only this labor and delivery takes years. Gulp.

I am reminded of my birthing classes and the delivery room advice my instructor gave me when I was pregnant with my daughter: "Go with the pain—let it wash over you. Don't fight it." Although Lamaze doesn't work for our emotional contractions as we now give birth to adults (could you imagine doing that puffy breathing thing for six to eight years?), the advice still holds. The good news is that the similarity doesn't end there—as one experienced mom, Meredith L., whose daughter is now thirty told me: "As with childbirth, the pangs of having an adolescent are quickly forgotten." So *that's* why my mother remembers me as being "a joy" as a teenager.

But while it's a birth, it can also feel like a death. Says Shelley, "When Paige hit adolescence and she began to move away from me, I compared it to losing someone in death. Many aspects of her younger personality have disappeared, and it's been such a grieving process for me. This beautiful close relationship we had was gone—it was almost as if overnight someone else came to live in my house. I remember saying to people, 'I'm so depressed, I feel like I lost my kid.'"

Letting Go

One of the most helpful things you can do to facilitate the letting-go process, which is essentially just another name for the mother's act of separating from her own daughter and from her role as "Mommy" to a little kid, is to realize that your child is not (and never has been) you or an expression of you in any way. She is a distinct individual, and the sooner you accept that fact and let her know that it's okay with you—through your nonjudgmental actions and attitudes toward your differences—the sooner she will be able to move up one more rung on the ladder to adulthood without the nagging guilt of somehow disappointing her mother.

As well as being one of the more helpful things you can do right now, it's also one of the hardest because it's tied up with all the hopes and dreams you've had for your kid ever since she splattered paint on paper and you were convinced she was an absolute genius (oh, admit it—we've all thought that). Even if you swore to yourself, as I did, that you would never tell your daughter who to be, you can't help planning her life.

As with many areas involving adolescence, this is a murky one because there are some important aspects of a kid's life that we should plan—her schooling, for example, or for some, religious training—all of which are going to reflect our own values. We need to set limits and goals and decide a lot of things for them (for example, which camp is best), and we start doing it when they're tiny—before we even know who they really are.

So when it comes time to peel ourselves away from them, it's often difficult to know where our children end and our dreams and assumptions about them begin. The sad fact is that most of us, when we were pregnant, wanted a little version of ourselves, but it's high time we got off that notion because it can drive a kid nuts, as well as make her feel unsure about who she really is.

Smotherhood

Although "smotherhood" seems to be a problem for all of us, except the most self-aware, it reaches epidemic proportions with the Clueless and Best Bud Moms. A Clueless or Best Bud Mom, by definition, is a little hazy about the need for her child to separate in the first place, so being conscious of keeping her vision of herself apart from her vision of her child is a little advanced for her.

Although Clueless and Best Bud share this blind spot, the manifestations of it are very different. Mrs. Clueless, I believe, has a view of her kid, and nothing's going to change it. Since that view oftentimes includes seeing her teen as still a very dependent child, it makes sense that she wouldn't want it challenged or the premise of her relationship with her daughter would crumble. She knows what's best for her child, and no one is going to tell her otherwise, least of all her child.

You probably know the type—the one who forces her little one to take ballet or gymnastics, and the kid does it just to please Mommy (forget about herself). Eventually this woman impresses on her child how important it is to Mom for her to go to a particular college, never mind that it's the kid who has to spend four years there while Mom gets a nifty sticker for the rear window of her car. Clueless has to tumble to the truth—her daughter's not her, so she can't use her to relive her own life or make up for what was wrong in her own childhood.

Another Clueless Mom mistake is not recognizing when it's time to stop doing everything for her kid. If she's spent twelve years or so protecting her, helping her, and saving her from her own mistakes, it's going to be hard for her to down-shift her behavior now that her daughter's reached adolescence. But as Shelley N. said to me, "We moms have got to get out of the rescue game."

The Best Bud Version

Best Bud Mom has a different approach. She impedes her daughter's separation by sticking onto her like a leech in hot pants. Whereas Clueless acts as if her daughter is an extension of herself, Best Bud does the opposite: She acts as if *she* is an extension of her daughter. They do everything together—they dress alike, listen to the same music, gossip together—in fact, the Best Bud Mom is hard to shake. And the subliminal message that she actually sends is not so much that she loves her daughter, but that she needs her. And if she needs her that much, it suggests that she will not be able to survive emotionally without being a part of her child's life. That's an awesome responsibility for any kid to bear, not to mention terribly guilt-producing.

By glomming onto her daughter's life, teen culture, and friends, the Best Bud Mom is robbing her of the right to her independence and that necessary and glorious feeling of having her own special little world that no one in the family shares. At the end of separation, when she is finally an independent individual, she will move out of the community of her family altogether and into that special world. As we know, such a fundamental change is difficult enough as it is; imagine how hard it is when you have your mother running after you, or moving in lockstep with you, appropriating everything that you thought was solely your own.

The Uncool Way

Accepting that your little sweetie is a distinct person in her own right and letting her have her own world without squelching it or inviting yourself into it is the path of the Uncool Mom. When she needs to be different, let her go. Uncool Mom recognizes that aspects of her daughter's character that might have been true at age six do not necessarily survive to adolescence: Girls outgrow interests, tastes, and other parts of themselves the same way they outgrow shoes, and it can be even more expensive. (Any mom who has signed up her National Velvet–obsessed daughter for nonrefundable horseback riding lessons two days before the little darling decides that horses are dorky knows what I mean.) Most important, Ms. Uncool appreciates that her daughter will never and should never be a carbon copy of herself.

"When Danielle was little, I had a hard time accepting the fact that she's not a go-getter, like me," says Beth C. "At birthday parties she'd be the last one to collect the piñata candy or the last one to claim an instrument during a Miss Susie Sing-along, so she always ended up with the worst stuff. It really didn't matter to her, but it drove me nuts. I wanted her to be aggressive, but it's just not her."

Beth eventually dealt with the situation: "Over the years I've come to terms with it and accepted that she's not me. She's fourteen now, and when I give her advice, I always start by saying, 'This is what I would do, but you have to handle it your own way.'"

Spread the Love

Along with being used to doing everything for our daughters, we may also be used to being the center of their universe, and that's a really hard one to let go of. Even though it puts us in the weird position of having to fire ourselves, it's important that our daughters know that there are people close to them, other than their moms, whom they can rely on as they grow up.

I realized this year that when my daughter is having trouble with a boy, sometimes I'm not the best person to help her since I am as much at a loss about what makes a junior high school boy tick as I was when I was in junior high. So I recommend to her the advice of someone who once was a junior high boy—her dad. He is able to give her perspective on the situation—how boys can be nervous about sex and sexuality at this age—and because it comes from him (a guy) and not me (a nonguy), it works.

Mothers are so used to being the Band-Aid, the cure-all, the magic wand, that it's easy to be threatened when their girls get their comfort elsewhere. You can't be the *only* source of emotional support in her life—others are just as important (as long as one of the others isn't a twenty-six-year-old greasy biker named Hatchet who wears more leather than a Holstein.) You should be there for her when she needs you, but never try to *make* her need you or try to be all things to her.

Passing the Baton

Allowing other people to be valuable in your daughter's life is one of the first steps in accepting the fact that your role is diminishing. Of course she will rely on her dad, her teachers, her grandparents or aunt as well as you, but soon her friends will assume a position of importance that, like it or not, can be powerful. They may even play a part in your daughter's fledgling identity as a new person, one who, like you, she is just beginning to get to know.

Oftentimes adolescents figure out who they are by first figuring out who they are *not*, and unfortunately for us, we (the moms) are the first people they turn to—not to seek advice from, but to reject. Many animals as newborns go through a stage called imprinting. When they open their eyes for the first time, the being they see at that moment will be imprinted on their little minds as "Mommy" and thus embraced. Human teenagers go through sort of a reverse imprinting: As they emerge as a new person, the first being they see (Mom) they reject and put through all sorts of misery. They reject us not only as authority figures, but also as people. We did the same, and continue to do the same, to our mothers. (For example, have you ever been horrified when you start seeing your mother in yourself? I thought so.)

We all remember saying things to our parents like, "I hate you" or "You're old—you don't know what you're talking about." We swore that when we were parents we would never be like them, yet we are more like them than we ever thought possible.

"I Hate You!"

So there it is—they love us and they hate us. And you probably feel the same way toward them sometimes. A parenting lecturer once said to Shelley N., "If you can say no to these three questions—Do you like your child? Do you enjoy being with your child? Do you like how your child is acting lately?—then you know your child has hit adolescence."

My daughter has said to me, "I'm not supposed to have fun with my mother," as well as, "I don't know what's wrong with me but I actually like you today." I know that since she is only thirteen, it's just the beginning. I'm sure many of you have heard much worse, including the all-time classic "I hate you."

It's important when you hear those words that you keep some perspective and don't crumble. From what I understand, the first time is the worst, and if you maintain your composure, the subsequent "I hate you's" get so watered down, it's almost like she's just saying hi. It's also important to remember the pain that they are going through and to try to muster your compassion for them even in the face of verbal abuse. "I hate you" can mean other things, such as frustration. Following is a table outlining some of the actual things your confused teen may be thinking when she utters those three little words.

And They're Off . . .

I think I'm ready for what adolescence will bring, whether it's inexplicable crying jags followed immediately by the giggles, or hellacious fights over clothes while shopping at the mall followed immediately by her dying to have a warm and friendly chat on the way home. I'm securely strapped into my seat bracing myself for all the hairpin turns of my daughter's personal

Teen Talk Translation Table #1

What she says	What she means
I hate you.	I'm very confused about what's happening to me and my body.
I hate you.	I'm bored and I want to get a rise out of you.
I hate you.	I'm embarrassed by what I just did to get in trouble and can't admit it.
I hate you.	I know someday I'll appreciate you, but right now this is the only fun I get.
I hate you.	I'm mad at the world and you're the closest target.
I hate you.	I want to be alone.
I hate you.	This is the best way I know to hurt you.
I hate you.	I'm scared and I really need a hug, but I'm too proud to say so.
I hate you.	I hate you.

roller coaster ride. Now at thirteen, she's confused. She's afraid to be too dependent and not "teenage" enough, but she still needs me. She knows she should be rejecting me, but she doesn't want to hate me. Well, she'll get over it.

Regardless of what form her rebellion takes, I will keep my Uncool eye on the thing that really matters—what this rebellion is all about: her separation from me. And when things get really tough, I hope to remind myself that I owe it to her to let her be a typical teenager. After all, we enjoyed rejecting our parents and making their lives miserable; why should we deprive our kids of the same pleasure? Separation may be painful, but it's necessary, and in the end, we'll both be better off for it.

And I know that in thirty years she'll be horrified that she's turning into me.

Dr. Ava says:

Your teenager has five developmental tasks to accomplish in the years that bridge childhood and adulthood—she's got to psychologically separate from her family, forge new ties among her peers, open herself to new ideas and new ideals, develop a sexual identity and initiate a sexual life, and wind up with a mature personality and good character. (In other words, she's got a lot on her plate.)

In this chapter, we're discussing the first and foremost of these tasks—**psychological separation.** Adolescence will be much less annoying, angering, and anxiety producing if you understand that many of your daily conflicts actually reflect your daughter's attempts (however obnoxious they may seem) to loosen the ties that bind her to you.

But separation, like attachment, is a two-way street; the emotional traffic has to flow in both directions. Your daughter has the advantage of pubertal hormonal changes to boost her from "baby" to "babe," but you'll need to rely on your knowledge of adolescent development to become the mom your teen needs now—a mom who is able to relinquish some of the psychic power you've accumulated all throughout her childhood.

One of the hardest jobs you face as your daughter matures is knowing exactly how to negotiate that fine line between *overexposing* her to challenges she's not yet ready to master and *overprotecting* her, depriving your daughter of the opportunity to build important skills. The Best Bud Mom falls down on her job as a parent because she doesn't recognize that her daughter's needs are different from her own, while the Clueless Mom is likely to infantilize her daughter and undermine her maturity and competence. But here are some things you (The Uncool Mom) can do that will help your daughter succeed at separating from you in a healthy way:

1. **Let go of your need to be admired or adored.** Teenagers reserve their adoration for pop stars and their admiration for peers, and that's as it should be. This is the time they knock you off your pedestal.

2. **Stay firm and steady in the face of your teen's emotional upheavals.** Adolescence repeats the struggles for independence of the toddler years, including the tantrums. (Remember "Me do it!" "Mommy, go away" "No need help!"?) But remember, you don't have to relinquish your *authority* in order to give your daughter some *autonomy*.

3. **Acknowledge that you and your daughter are different people from different generations.** She's going to be around long after you've gone, so helping her separate from you *now* enables her to find someone to love in her own generation *later*. (The saddest thing I've ever heard was from a teenage girl who told me, "My mom is my idol. I just want to stay with her forever.")

4. **Let go of the idea that "Mommy can kiss it and make it better."** The kinds of problems your teenage daughter now faces require your *sympathy* and *support* rather than your *solutions*. The whole point of the teenage years is to give your daughter some time and space to learn how to get along in life without you.

5. Clothes and Shopping

I'm only interested in clothes that are worn
in beer commercials.
—Sabrina, 14

My Waterloo

Just about any mom who has a teen daughter can tell you about a specific moment when she knew that adolescence with all its baggage of frustration and misery had arrived for a long uninvited stay. For me that moment came when my daughter and I were clothes shopping—often the teen's first foray into adolescent rebellion.

Now, I can't say that all of our previous shopping excursions had been pure pleasure, but those disagreements were simply the result of two very strong-willed people locked in mortal combat about things like washability, proper sizing (she hated having to grow into things; I hated having her grow out of things), and whether she could wear a pearl-encrusted First Communion dress to school (we're not even Catholic). But this—this was much worse.

We were visiting my in-laws at the time, and I thought that a nice mother-daughter-grandmother shopping trip would be a good activity to do together and a way to get her back-to-school wardrobe to boot. We all enjoy fashion, so it should be fun, right? Yeah, right.

The Value of Personal Style

Before I go into the details, it's important to know that very rarely did my daughter and I argue over taste. Ever since she was tiny, she had a very definite and somewhat quirky style, which I encouraged since I've always seen personal adornment as a valuable means of self-expression. If it made her happy at age four to wear pants with a dress and mix plaid with zebra stripes, who was I to thwart her?

Besides, self-expression is vital for a child to become her own person and to feel confident in her own choices. It's easy for a mother to send a mixed message when she forces her children to conform to her sense of what looks good and then when they reach the teen years tell them to assert their individuality and not to succumb to peer pressure. If individuality is good when they get older, then help them foster it when they are still young.

The Battle

The three of us (my daughter, my mother-in-law, and I) gamely walked into a branch of my daughter's favorite (at the time) chain store. My mother-in-law, Helen, a wonderful woman who contradicts the stereotype of the pushy relative, hung back and stayed out of the way. Had I been a bit more observant, I would have asked why and saved myself from the train wreck that was waiting to happen.

I charged into the shopping fray and started pulling out various tops and pants and skirts that I absolutely *knew* my daughter would love. I prided myself on being such a great (uh-oh—cool?) mom that I was right on my kid's wavelength style-wise. I wasn't going to force her to wear what I liked; I was going to force her to wear what she liked, or what I presumed she liked. Either way, I was sticking my nose into an area of her life that she wanted to control. I think that how kids dress—how they choose to present themselves to the world—is one of the first ways they define themselves and declare their independence from us, and my daughter was no exception.

The store was filled with the kind of funky, '70s-inspired clothes that she had recently been favoring. Shootin' fish in a barrel. But as I blithely presented her with my selections, she bristled. Rejection. What was going on? I followed her through the racks, watching and waiting to see what she would pick up. When she expressed enthusiasm for an embroidered top, I chimed in, "Oh, that's cute." She immediately put it back. Unable to comprehend why she would so suddenly change her mind, I took it off the rack again and reiterated how nice it was.

"I just don't like it," she said.

"But you liked it two minutes ago. Besides, it goes with your blue skirt."

"I hate that skirt."

"No, you don't."

Then she hit me with one of the most withering cannonballs in the teenage arsenal: "Mo-o-om!" drawing it out to three syllables and instantaneously branding me as an object of scorn for all to see. I couldn't escape it—I was a mother of a contemptuous teen in a store filled with a bunch of women with adoring daughters. She might as well have forced me to wear a Scarlet *M*.

A Word to the Unwise

Having just temporarily immobilized me, my daughter scooted off alone. I turned to Helen. "Did you see that? Was it me? What did I do?" She looked at me with the sympathetic wisdom that only someone who has survived many teen battles has. Then she bestowed upon me this pearl: "Remove yourself from the conflict."

Quickly, before my daughter reappeared, she elaborated: "Don't get involved in selecting specific outfits. If there are clothes you want her to consider or clothes that you disapprove of, enlist the salesgirls to help you. They can advise for or against a particular garment far more effectively than a mother can. Salesgirls make young teens feel grown-up; mothers make them feel like babies. And most importantly," she concluded, "never, ever give an opinion. Stay neutral and show no enthusiasm. If necessary, if you really like something, tell her you hate it—she's bound to love it that way." Fantastic advice—all Uncool.

Power Struggles

Being difficult about clothes and asserting their sartorial tastes seem to be, for many girls, their first foray into typically adolescent behavior—their first step on the journey that leads them to discover who they really are—apart from us. They start to challenge us on many things, but clothes seem to be the most obvious lightning rod, which may have to do with the power of clothing in determining social groups in school (social groups that are growing in importance in their lives just as our importance is beginning to fade). But it could also be a favorite point of rebellion because for many moms and daughters, shopping was a fun, pleasant, and bonding experience during early childhood.

How many of us weren't thrilled when the doctor announced, "It's a girl!" Wasn't it easier to get through messy diapers and unexplained crying jags (from the baby, not you) by fantasizing about all the pretty little dresses and cute outfits you were going to put her in as soon as she learned not to vomit so often? And admit it: We all dreamed of having a girl we could dress like a princess, and we probably all have even gazed at wedding dresses thinking, "Some day…." Well, I maintain that on some level our girls know this about us, and it's the first toe of ours they think of stepping on.

Of course, there's another aspect as well. The girls probably found early childhood shopping trips with Mommy when she would buy them pretty things and have lunch or a snack together as fairly special too. To find themselves, they must reject us; to reject us, they must reject the experiences between mother and daughter that have been special to them. How many times when you've gone shopping with your teen have the words, "Mom, I'm not a baby anymore" come out? It's a classic power struggle: They want the power over their lives, and we're loathe to hand over the reins all at once. Only instead of a picket line, they show their protest through their clothes.

Shop 'til You're Dropped

A fine example of this dynamic is reflected in the experiences of Uncool Mom Valerie B. and her daughter Caroline, now thirteen who had had many pleasurable years of shopping together with Caroline's Aunt Trisha. But the specter of adolescence hung in the air around the happy threesome and decided to crash-land onto Caroline's shoulder at the local Nordstrom. "I

Diagram of a Shopping Trip with a Teen

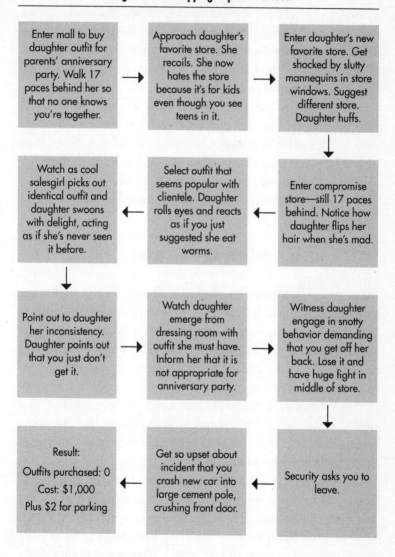

Enter mall to buy daughter outfit for parents' anniversary party. Walk 17 paces behind her so that no one knows you're together. →

Approach daughter's favorite store. She recoils. She now hates the store because it's for kids even though you see teens in it. →

Enter daughter's new favorite store. Get shocked by slutty mannequins in store windows. Suggest different store. Daughter huffs.

↓

Watch as cool salesgirl picks out identical outfit and daughter swoons with delight, acting as if she's never seen it before. ←

Select outfit that seems popular with clientele. Daughter rolls eyes and reacts as if you just suggested she eat worms. ←

Enter compromise store—still 17 paces behind. Notice how daughter flips her hair when she's mad.

↓

Point out to daughter her inconsistency. Daughter points out that you just don't get it. →

Watch daughter emerge from dressing room with outfit she must have. Inform her that it is not appropriate for anniversary party. →

Witness daughter engage in snotty behavior demanding that you get off her back. Lose it and have huge fight in middle of store.

↓

Result:

Outfits purchased: 0

Cost: $1,000

Plus $2 for parking ←

Get so upset about incident that you crash new car into large cement pole, crushing front door. ←

Security asks you to leave.

picked out some cute outfits for her as I always did," said Valerie, "but when I showed them to her, she said, 'Mom, they'll kill me.' It hit me by surprise. For the first time she was being defined not by what I put on her but by her peers. 'They'll kill me.' And I thought: who are 'they'? And how do they have this power over you now?"

Not only do our girls need to reject us through the shopping experience, but also they need to reject those clothes that we select for them as a way of negating our influence over their identities. They want to repudiate our view of them so that they can get to determine their own new identities, which will have nothing to do with their old identities as our babies.

What to Do, What to Do?

Once you're enmeshed in clothes shopping battles with your teen, it's very difficult to get out of the cycle. Even though it isn't a pleasant experience for either of you (Suzanne A. says of her daughter, "I would rather go through childbirth than take her shopping"), there seems to be a strange compulsion to continue, regardless of how many times you vow, even as you're riding up the escalator, not to get into another tussle. I have found that the Uncool Mom approach to surviving the Shopping Wars generally consists of two strategies, both borrowing from the Helen Solution of removing yourself from the conflict.

One method of removing yourself from the conflict is doing just that—removing yourself. Take a step back physically and mentally, disengage from the struggle, and simply opt out. Your first reaction may be, "But that's just giving up! I can't let my kid win!" For those of you who entertained that thought, I offer you a story that, although it may seem like a detour, is actually quite germane.

The Seemingly Irrelevant Story

At one point in seventh grade, my daughter was caught up in a dirty-look/snide-comment feud with some other girls in her school. It had reached a point, as all feuds do, where no one could determine who had started it so that each additional insult was interpreted as an aggressive rather than retaliatory act by either side. The end result was a Möbius strip of adolescent contempt. Apparently, neither side was willing to be the first to lay down arms (or in this case, curled upper lips and rolled eyeballs) because of the fear that the other side would be victorious. "I can't let them win!" she told me.

I likened the battle she was having with these girls to a tug-of-war: one side pulling, the other pulling back harder. The only way one side could win with any satisfaction would be by pulling the opposing side into the mud between them.

But if she let go of the rope—opting out and removing herself from the conflict—the fight would be over with no one actually winning. She could walk away proudly, knowing that the conflict was a waste of time and had no inherent value. She thought it made sense.

I continued, "It's sort of like this old hippie slogan from the '60s during Vietnam: What if they gave a war and no one came?" I nodded wisely and waited for her response.

"You grew up in a dorky time."

The Point

I've taken my own advice and have dropped the rope in the shopping tugs-of-war that I had been having with my daughter. It's not a question of my losing and her winning because it's not a fight worth having. Besides, it's my job as an Uncool Mom to relinquish little bits of power to her now and again. Considering what lies ahead in teendom, shopping is a gimme.

I now, à la Helen, let the salesgirls help. I allow her relatively free rein to express herself sartorially, never offer an opinion, and refuse to be reeled into arguments. These days when I go on shopping trips with her, I know that the chances are good that she might choose a color or style that's not the most flattering, but I try not to care. It helps if I pretend I'm on nitrous oxide.

Another Technique

When her daughter Alex was thirteen or so, Janice H. had a miserable time shopping with her. Often their fights were about money—how much Alex could spend on birthday gifts for her friends, or how many items Alex was going to get for herself.

Janice developed a system. Before she and Alex left the house, she would set out a game plan. "I would say, 'You can spend x amount, and that's it." I refused to get caught up in what everyone else was spending. That way, by the time we got there, we didn't have to have any discussions that could turn into fights, and she knew ahead of time that I wasn't going to pay for anything more."

Tactic Number Two

What do commanders do when their troops have been fighting and are too exhausted or distressed to continue? Call in the reinforcements. The reinforcement in our house is Dad (for others it can be a grandparent, aunt, or friend). Sometimes, when even opting out became a tense shopping experience (girls can sometimes be very clever and tireless in their attempts to get under our skin), I send her out with Dad. Not only do they have a pleasant time together, they actually bring home things that she needed.

Just be careful that Dad pays attention to what your daughter selects before the credit card comes out so that there are no surprises for Mom when they get home, like a school wardrobe that looks like it belongs to a Dallas Cowboys cheerleader.

A New Identity

Clothing and shopping not only present to adolescent girls a fantastic opportunity to start up the dissension that is so necessary as they separate from their mothers, but also give them a chance to start defining themselves by their own sense of who they are. Our choice equals our image of them; thus they push that aside to develop their own identity represented by their own style—a style that we may not agree with and most likely don't understand.

No longer do they want us to be the ones who know them better than anyone else does—they're reserving that honor for themselves. So they dress in a way that says, "So there. Thought you knew me, didn't you? Well I'm a new person now, and I'm not who you think I am." They want to be in control of establishing their own identities and we're not invited to weigh in on them. If we do, we run the risk of their going in the opposite direction to make sure they're as different from us as humanly possible.

How to Cope

First, let's look at the way our fellow moms, Mrs. Clueless and Ms. Best Bud, tend to handle this frustrating experience. The Clueless Mom, in constant denial that it's time for her dear little girl to grow up, will keep a tight hold on the reins of her daughter's wardrobe, preventing any kind of sartorial mutiny from taking place. She might think that she has kept the tide of rebellious youth at bay, but in fact she is simply building a dam—a very temporary and probably flimsy one that might hold the turbulence for a short time, but might crumble under the growing pressure later on, leaving a stressed-out and hostile older child to deal with the damage. Not good.

And how does the Best Bud Mom attack the situation? She doesn't. She allows her daughter to do whatever she wants to do regardless of how suggestive (and thus dangerous) her outfits might be. It's one thing to opt out of the battle; it's quite another to relinquish all responsibility as a parent. In fact, Best Bud might even join her daughter in her quest for the sluttiest or pop-star-trendiest attire.

Mom's Rules of Appropriate Attire

Fully aware of my daughter's strong fashion opinions since she was three and insisted on wearing two dresses (one over the other) to school, I devised a set of rules that have helped us agree on what she is allowed to wear to what. Even though we've had our share of battles in the dressing rooms of nearly every major department store in the New York metropolitan area, once the clothes are home, we almost never have conflicts about how she should dress for a particular event. These rules are very simple and, at least so far, have managed to keep peace in the house while allowing her to feel good about what she's wearing.

1. *The outfit must be appropriate for the weather*—If she wants to wear a tank top in January, she must bring some kind of covering: sweater, sweatshirt, etc. If it's the middle of summer, I'm less concerned. If she wants to sweat to death, fine.
2. *The outfit must be appropriate for the occasion*—no sequins just to go watch her little brother play Little League. And conversely, no shorts and tank tops at a nice holiday brunch.
3. *The outfit must be appropriate for her age*—She knows that I am not going to allow her to leave the house dressed like a twenty-year-old extra from *Chicago*. Periodically she tries to push the envelope, but ultimately she's been pretty reasonable. When it comes to school attire, I let the school be the heavy with their dress code.

This system has been successful in my house because by following it my daughter gets something in return: I don't question any fashion judgment that falls within the rules—she can express herself in her clothing as much as she wants, as long as she stays within the boundaries. We both give a little and we both get a little.

The Challenges Ahead

The last rule is the most difficult to enforce because what would be considered appropriate for a girl's age is so subjective. Of all the rules, number three is the one that she challenges me on because at times it seems as though I'm going backward. A little girl dressed in tight leggings and top looks like a puppy; a pubescent girl with a blossoming figure and a newly curvy butt dressed the same way looks like a streetwalker. So she gets annoyed when I say she must dress in less revealing things the older she gets.

These debates usually end in a conversation about how teenage girls often have a sexual power they don't know the strength of and have no idea how to handle. They're too young to understand the messages that they send because in the early teen years they're still sort of playing dress-up and don't yet understand how boys interpret their actions. A girl dressed in something that she thinks makes her look like Shakira may just want to be admired from afar, whereas the boy might look at her choice of attire and think it means "Come and get me!"

Every year when she goes away to camp (where I can't enforce my rules—drat!), I have this same discussion with her. I try to get her to remember this one caveat about how she chooses to dress: Don't advertise anything that you're not willing to sell. Boys get angry when there's a bait-and-switch.

But this experience will prove no different from the rest of the challenges we have to face as we bring up a teen. It's much harder to do things the Uncool way because it requires a lot of time, effort, and thought—usually after a long day when our brains are in hibernation mode. Life with an adolescent girl is a constant negotiation (clothes are really only part of it) because that's what it takes to hand over the reins gradually so that by the time they reach adulthood and are in control, they'll be ready, and you'll be too tired to care if they dress like a bagwoman, a safety-pinned punk, or a Las Vegas showgirl.

Our Closets

No chapter on this topic could be complete without at least a brief exploration of the Best Buds' penchant to dress in the same styles as their daughters as well as the Best Bud land mines that await the rest of us as we try to be stylish and attractive while being good moms—and age at the same time.

It's easy to get caught up in the youth culture in this country, especially if you've kept in shape and have ignored the fact that you've aged the same number of years that your daughter has since she was born. But recognizing those years and the physical changes that they bring can safeguard you against looking like an idiot.

But don't take my word for it—listen to Kayla, seventeen, whose mom, Diane F., lets us in on her daughter's observations of our generation. "Kayla does make comments when she sees women my age (over forty) and much older dressing as if they were her buddy. She thinks it's sad when she sees women dressing like teenagers."

Act Your Age, Not Your Steve Madden Shoe Size

During the writing of this book my daughter has had more than a few criticisms, but one of her biggest objections is that she thinks that I am insisting that all mothers "dress like nuns." "No," I've explained, "they can look attractive without looking like a teenager." At an age where she really only finds teens and young people in their early twenties attractive, she was not enthusiastic about my rebuttal, but I hold steadfast in my belief that one can age and look good at the same time without grossing anyone out.

How do I dress? I like to think I'm casual yet smart, chic yet not trendy, and most of all, age-appropriate yet not frumpy. At any age you can dress with elegance and, if you're a bit braver, flair or wit. I have a jacket made of appliquéd fabric leaves (it's better than it sounds), but I don't own a single tube top, a skirt so short that it almost shows my episiotomy scar, or jeans so low that I need a Brazilian wax just to wear them to the grocery store.

I'm in my mid-forties. I stay relatively fit, and I like to look nice. But I no longer need to be in the spotlight the way I did when I was in my twenties. I had that fun. I am no longer a pretty young thing—and that's okay, because pretty young things also have pretty crummy entry-level jobs and pretty steep car insurance premiums and pretty big worries about getting married to their pretty noncommittal boyfriends in their pretty young heads. If you want the stability and perspective that age gives you, you've got to age.

Do It for the Children

In other words, try not to get caught up in the youth culture Best Bud trap of dressing like a teen. If for no other reason, do it for your daughter's sake. When you were her age, would you have wanted to shop at the same store, in the same department as your mother? Would you have liked to come out of a dressing room in the latest hip-hugger bell-bottoms, only to see your mother emerge from the next stall similarly appareled? 'Nuff said.

So try to keep your wardrobe and your daughter's wardrobe apart. And if you notice that she continually asks to borrow your clothes, then you have to wonder if it means you've got the wrong clothes, unless she wants them for a Halloween costume.

And if, after all this, the urge to dress like a teenager becomes uncontrollable, I have one word for you: Cher.

Dr. Ava says:

At least two important battles are fought in the Adolescent Clothes Wars. The first battle is about your daughter's need to establish herself as her own person with her own ideas (even if they are wrong!). Your opinions will inevitably be shot down because the whole point of this skirmish is to strengthen *her* and diminish you.

The second battle in the Clothes Wars has a more hidden subtext, which goes something like this: "Now that I have my period, I'm the new queen. You're on your way down the ladder of sexual desirability, and I'm on my way up." In other words, during adolescence your daughter naturally and normally tries both to identify with you as a woman *and* to compete with you. That's why many of the fights over clothes are about outfits that are either too revealing or too suggestive for your taste. Your daughter is asserting her new capacity to be sexy. And while this is a word that strikes terror in your heart, don't forget that in many cultures in the world, a twelve-year-old is already considered marriage material.

What makes all of this particularly confusing for us is that our culture can't seem to decide what it wants girls to do. On the one hand, we market bare midriffs, platform shoes, and tight miniskirts to nine-year-olds, boosting early sexual awareness. On the other hand, we encourage girls to focus on their careers and delay both marriage and motherhood. This double message extends adolescence at both ends of the spectrum. Girls (who do physically mature one to two years earlier in this generation) are becoming and acting like adolescents by the time they're ten years old, but at the other end, they're not taking on the responsibilities that help to transform them into adults until well into their thirties.

This extended adolescence means more conflicts and competition to deal with over a longer period of time. A wise (Uncool) mom doesn't ignore the complicated meanings of the Clothes Wars (as a Clueless Mom might do), nor does she actively compete with her teen, (as the Best Bud Mom does). Instead, she steps in to discuss and implement reasonable clothing parameters with her daughter ("Mom's Rules of Appropriate Attire" is a good place to start), and then she steps out, leaving room for her daughter to create and clothe the kind of young woman she wants to be. (Believe me, it's a whole lot easier to tolerate a sparkly turquoise tube top than a teenage conversion to Hare Kishna.)

6. Public Behavior—
Hers and Yours

Don't touch me—the popular girls are watching!
—Lizzy, 13

The Teen Reconnaissance Mission

Since my daughter turned eleven, she has hated having anyone she knows to see us together in public. The sheer possibility of it generates visible panic in her face. Am I particularly revolting? Do I have matted hair growing in places where only subprimates have it? Am I prone to periodic blackouts during which I engage in fits of drooling and screaming like a banshee at innocent children passing by? Not since my own middle school years have I been so ruthlessly shunned—and it's happening again, this time by my own flesh and blood.

Yes, by my daughter—the same one whom I unflinchingly stood by a good ten years ago when she had mortifying tantrums in public and joyously shouted out scatological details when in fine dining establishments. How quickly they forget.

So now, whenever we are going somewhere together, she

scopes out the environs while still in the car, trying to determine if anyone she knows is lurking about and ready to do God-knows-what if they see her with—gasp—her mother. If we go to the mall, she does a 360-degree survey of the place, scouting for any other middle school–aged girls, and then moves warily from store to store, her popular girl antenna up and quivering. One of her favorite methods of avoiding detection is to vigorously charge ahead, thus forcing me to follow ten paces behind like an eighteenth-century Japanese wife. This unrelenting fear of discovery is something I associate more with carrying on an illicit affair, not going on a trip to the market with your mom, but then again, I'm not a teen.

Take Nothing Personally

Nothing illustrates the need for and the process of separation quite like an adolescent's revulsion to being seen with her mom. I realize that with each slight, she is physically and literally rejecting me. But that's okay because I try to remember the cardinal Uncool rule about teen behavior toward a parent: *Take nothing personally*. And as much as she has rules for me— Byzantine rules that stipulate when and where I can touch her or kiss her (I can kiss her forehead or the top of her head, but if I drift to her cheek, there's hell to pay)—I also have rules for her. I let her know that although I'm a pretty good sport about being considered as emotionally sensitive to her contempt as an effigy, she is not allowed to abuse me or my goodwill.

It's a tough balancing act—allowing her to reject me while keeping her attitude from venturing into disrespect—but it's one we all have to work on because few girls get through adolescence without wishing their moms would fall into a hole the minute they see their peers.

Mother–Daughter T-Shirts for Public Outings

Teen   Mom

See No Mother; Hear No Mother

Often the teen will expect certain behavior from her mother, just as my daughter expects me to abide by her no-kiss law. There are usually proscriptions against any form of personal warmth—no touching, no walking side by side, no personal chitchat (only absolutely necessary communication is allowed). These are obscure rules for an austere religion: Orthodox Adolescencism. And sometimes the canon can be pretty severe.

Just a few short years ago, Alex (then thirteen) considered her mother, Janice H., to be just a wallet with a bad hairdo. "She was humiliated to go with me to Bloomingdale's," remembers Janice, "because I didn't have the right 'look'—wrong hairdo, no manicure, no designer clothing. She said to me, 'You're just embarrassing to be with in Bloomingdale's' She didn't want anyone to know that I was her mom until it came time to pay. It was an awful period, but I held the line about my appearance. I would never change the way I look just to please her."

Be Yourself

Janice has it exactly right. Remaining who you are and not submitting to the whims of a teenager is absolutely imperative when dealing with these little tornadoes we gave birth to over a decade ago. In the midst of the emotional chaos that hallmarks the life of an adolescent, it is our job to remain calm and as solid and steadfast as Gibraltar during the throes of a rampaging storm. It is this reliability and strength that gives them the security to challenge you and grow.

When a mother makes changes in her appearance or behavior in order to please her kid, she comes across as weak and certainly not the steady rock of consistent authority her daughter needs to kick against. Trotting alongside like an obedient puppy and complying with her daughter's vision of who she should be for fear of being abandoned, she is doing her child a disservice. First, she's sacrificing her jurisdiction as the powerful boss-lady of the family, and second, she's interrupting the natural course of adolescence—i.e., the rejection of the parent as a stage of separation.

The Life of the Party

Trying to avoid the pain and disconnection of being jettisoned by their adolescent daughters, some mothers go the route of the Best Bud and, unlike Janice, do change to suit their daughters' moods and capricious demands. The Best Bud Mom insists on coming along when her teen engages in any sort of social frolic with her peers either because she is unable to admit that she is old enough to have a teen with a separate life, or because she can't stand running the risk of being told to "get lost," thereby losing her favorite companion. I'm sure for some there's a great deal of overlap in those two areas. The end result is a mom who acts her daughter's age and shifts into turbo-drive in her attempts to prove that she's cool enough to hang out with.

When her thirteen-year-old daughter Shannon came home after a party for her friend Jill, Cathy K. was slightly taken aback by Shannon's story of what transpired during this particular "teen night." Cathy recalls: "This mother sat with these teens through a movie in a theater, then watched a video with them at home, and even participated in the sleepover when the girls were gossiping about boys. She actually said, 'I am the coolest mom' several times throughout the night. Shannon said that all the girls were saying to her, 'Wouldn't you rather go to sleep?' but she just stayed put. The girls thought it was strange, and it must have been pretty embarrassing for her daughter."

We all know that once you have a kid, there are some things you can't do, such as leave your kid at home alone because you decided to have a spontaneous weekend away. You also give up a full night's sleep when they're infants (and then again when they start driving). It's a trade-off. If you want one thing in your life, you have to give something else up—that's what happens when you make a choice. You chose to be a parent. So when your daughter gets to the teenage years, you've got to give up the fantasy that you're still a hot babe in your twenties and that you're never going to get old.

The Public Face of Mrs. Clueless

On the other side of the spectrum of maternal public behavior lies the Clueless Mom. As in other facets of her life with a teen, her guiding star is the firm refusal to acknowledge that her daughter is growing up and away from her. She still sees her as her little girl, her baby, her own private property she can fuss with, tend to, and touch at will, resulting in all sorts of invasions of her daughter's personal space. Ignoring her child's fundamental shift toward independence, the Clueless Mom makes no adjustments in how she acts toward her in public, continuing to behave as if she still has the right to brush crumbs off the chin of her teenager in the middle of a restaurant.

Remember how when your child was born you did everything for her? It was virtually an automatic response. When her nose was running, you'd wipe it (and if there were no tissues available, your shirt or even your hand would do); when there was crusty sleep in her eyes, you'd pick it out; when her ears were accruing a waxy buildup, you'd swab them. There was no secretion too messy or too gross that you couldn't handle—even while eating.

Basic Instinct

Why do we do this? Because all of the sundry snot and slime originates from someone who is *your* baby—someone who was inside of you sharing meals and blood. It's that old maternal instinct we hear so much about. Unfortunately, that same instinct does not know how to take its cue and pack its bags and politely leave when our daughters reach the age of full-blown disdain for our loving touch. Too often it has to be forcibly evicted after we do something inexcusable like spontaneously fix a strand of our adolescent's hair prompting a combustive reaction that rivals that of two fuel tankers in a head-on collision. And even after that, our tenacious little instinct can periodically return for ill-advised visits.

Already having been chastened by my daughter for my repugnant and unnecessarily intrusive public displays of affection toward her, there are still times when I forget and my irrepressible instinct takes over. On a chilly winter day I was late picking her up from school. Knowing that she would be cold, worried, and distraught, I spent the drive there feeling terribly guilty that I would put her through such avoidable distress.

When I got there, I could see in her face how upset she was and immediately hugged her to apologize. In my arms she felt like ice—was she out in the cold that long? Then she spat out, "Get off! Don't you dare hug me at school." I then realized that her frostiness had nothing to do with the temperature—it was merely garden-variety teen mortification.

We all do it and we probably all have memories of our

mothers doing it (my mother used to straighten my eyebrows in public with spit-lubricated thumbs well into my teens, making me recoil in horror every time). But still, it's a Clueless impulse, which we should do everything in our power to quash. By not respecting our daughters' newfound independence, we're essentially dismissing their desires to grow up and sending the message that it displeases us. The motto for the woman with a young adolescent girl should be: Think before you kiss—the age of spontaneous affection is over.

The Goldilocks Paradigm

So if the Best Bud style ends up being all wrong at one extreme like Papa Bear, and the Clueless road leads to an equally uncomfortable result in the opposite direction like Mama Bear, then what public behavior model can assume the place of Baby Bear? You guessed it—the Uncool method. Whereas Best Bud is too embarrassing, and Mrs. Clueless is also too embarrassing, the Uncool Mom is just embarrassing enough.

In the venerable Baby Bear tradition, the Uncool approach is all about moderation. That middle ground, the Uncool Golden Mean, involves remaining true to yourself and not tailoring your behavior to suck up to anyone while reining in your most curious habits that may be unnecessarily humiliating to a sensitive teen (who, by the way, is positive that everyone at the mall is passing damning judgment on her for being seen with an overly strange mother). She's going to be embarrassed to be seen with you no matter what, so there's no need to gild the lily.

Be Polite

If you think about it, what I'm really advocating is common courtesy. You should consider your daughter's feelings before you engage in a particular behavior when you're with her in public, because that's what you would do if you were with your husband, friend, or coworker. Sure, I might like to sing "Muskrat Love" a little louder than I should while I'm food shopping by myself, but if I'm with someone whom that would discomfit, I can refrain because it's good manners. Once again, it's easy to make the mistake of not recognizing that your daughter is a person in her own right and not the little baby who was so much a part of you that you blithely took her with you to the toilet. You wouldn't do that now, so make sure the rest of your actions follow suit.

Only a rude, selfish, and small-minded narcissist would go about acting without regard for the feelings of others, someone sort of like, say, a teenage girl. Oh, well. This mothering business is rarely a two-way street. Since polite behavior that considers the comfort of others is a lesson we would all like our daughters to learn, wouldn't teaching it be a lot easier if we were practicing it first? How does this sound: "I'm just asking you to show me the same respect that I show you." It's nice to have that one up your sleeve.

Of course what your adolescent deems as polite conduct on your part may be very different from what you consider polite. I first decide what is reasonable, and then my daughter has to accept it, but I try very hard to be fair. Again, moderation is the key. For instance, saying hello to neighbors in a public place is reasonable—and it is unreasonable for her to be embarrassed by my civility; however, getting into an extended, gabby chinfest that includes laughing like a hyena in public I would classify as unnecessary and thus unreasonable. If you're with your daughter and you see a friend, limit your conversation to no more than five minutes, and while you're chatting, make arrangements to have coffee together without the kids. It's not an easy rule to follow, and I have a tendency to break it myself sometimes. When I do, I grant her the right to be annoyed at me, and I subsequently apologize.

"I'm sorry" is probably the least uttered phrase to kids by people who consider themselves strong parents, which is a shame. Apologizing to your child when you make a mistake, act unfairly, or behave inconsistently is hardly a sign of weakness; in fact, it shows that you're strong enough to admit when you're wrong and withstand whatever criticism may follow. It gives you a certain amount of credibility with your child that can come in handy later on. In addition, you are, by example, teaching your daughter how to acknowledge her own mistakes. You may not be able to enjoy the results of that lesson until she is no longer in your care, but it'll be nice for everyone else.

The Hunger

I've had plenty of opportunities to apologize to my daughter since, despite the fact that I have developed the Uncool philosophy, I still make plenty of mistakes. A year or so ago I was running around town trying to finish some tedious errands before having to pick up my daughter from her school play auditions. In order to make sure I wasn't late, I put off eating lunch, assuming that she and I could grab a bite on the way home. She had given me a precise time: 3:45—rather late for lunch, but I knew I could last that long.

I arrived right on time; she did not. I sat there growing ever hungrier and resentful that I had delayed much-needed nutrition so that I could waste away in my car with nothing to do but think about how empty my stomach was and how she was probably just hanging out with her friends. When I could stand it no longer, I burst out of my car and into the school, tearing my way to the auditorium. There she was, having fun. I lost it and started yelling at her in front of her friends about how rude she was not to come out on time and how I had sacrificed my lunch in order to pick her up on time. She defended herself: The auditions were taking longer than expected and earlier she had called me at home to tell me to come at 4:30. Unfortunately, I hadn't been at home all afternoon so I never got the message.

I used the rest of my waiting time to go grab a muffin. I ate it, and when my hunger pangs stopped, I immediately saw the error of my ways. Upon returning to the scene of the crime, I offered the apology that my daughter rightfully deserved. She had been truly mortified. She told me that her friends hated me and thought I was the worst mother in history. I stood there and took the blows.

On the way home, the dust settled and we were actually able to laugh about it. We made up funny stories to tell her friends to explain why I had suddenly acted like Baba Yaga, but I also let her know that she had the right to just say that I lost it and acted like a jerk for no good reason.

What did I learn from this experience? That I should never say anything to my daughter on an empty stomach unless it's "Oh good, the waitress is coming." Also, that had I not apologized, our ride home would have been filled with anger and bitterness from her and arrogant self-preservation from me instead of laughter from both of us.

The Flip Side of the Coin

So much for mom—what about the teenager's behavior in public? From talking to a good number of mothers, I would say that adolescent girls fall into one of two categories—the Stealth Bombers: those who reserve their worst behavior for the home where their family gets the full brunt of it, and the Daisy Cutters: those who let loose wherever and whenever they feel like it. As for the Stealth Bombers, they are always the ones you compliment to their mothers about what charming and poised young ladies they are only to receive an uncomprehending stare in return that is quickly followed by a snort, and then, "You should see her at home."

The Daisy Cutters display the public behavior that is more typically associated with teenagers: flippancy, moodiness, and hissy fits. These are the girls whose mothers get no compliments, only sympathetic looks from the women in the mall who have also braved the same battlefield.

If your daughter is a Daisy Cutter, it's important to remember to take nothing personally. She isn't behaving in some embarrassing way in public just to spite you. Actually, she is, but she would act like this no matter who her mother was. Your "motherness" is exactly what she finds so reprehensible, and to express her feelings, sometimes she treats you in a most irritating and demeaning manner.

Mother as Slave

Some teens enjoy embarrassing their moms by publicly putting them on the spot when they're with their friends. By demanding something of you when others are present, she expects to get away with that something because she assumes that you're less likely to be as strict or to squabble as you would in the safety of your own home.

"I drove my daughter and her friends into town to hang out with some other girls," says Robin B. "Eliza, who is four-teen, said to me very cavalierly, 'Mom, we need to be picked up at 3:00.' Now I was in front of this other mother as well as the girls and I knew my reaction was on display, but I said, 'No. You guys can walk home. I'm not a chauffeur.' I know she was embarrassed in front of her friends, but tough. I can't raise a child who has no regard for anyone but herself, and that impulse is much stronger than my desire to be liked by her friends."

Had Eliza asked her mom in a more polite manner, Robin might have tried to work something out. But she didn't, so Robin held firm. "This assumption that I'm at her beck and call really irritates me. I will not be a schlepper mother; I will not be a slave mother. Women who agree to that, who wait on their children hand and foot, ultimately they are afraid of their chil-dren—afraid of being hated. I can't stand that." What Robin describes here is the Best Bud fear of being rejected, and she correctly sees how that attitude can put the power in the family in the hands of the teenager.

Guttermouths

And then there's cursing. Judy L. approaches the issue head-on. "When I hear Lindsay or her friends slip and use words like *freakin'* or *sucks*, I correct them all the time and explain how horrible it sounds. I tell Lindsay that being a teenager is not an excuse for cursing because it may become a habit and slip out at the wrong times. I asked her how would she feel if I were at a parent/teacher conference and this is how I spoke to her teacher: 'Oh my, this really *sucks*. What kind of freakin' grade is this?' I believe it sinks in when I put it that way."

Practical Applications of the Rule of Moderation

Moderation can help you deal with almost all of your daughter's less than perfect behavior when she is out with you. For one, never force your daughter to accompany you on outings unless necessary. That strategy right there will cut down on a lot of public behavior stress. If you have to take her, let her bring a friend. They will keep each other occupied, which will reduce the number of opportunities your daughter will find to torture you.

On trips to the mall, if you're not ready to let her go on her own with friends, consider walkie-talkies, like Uncool Mom Denise J. It gives a teen a sense of independence while providing her mom with peace of mind. Just make sure they aren't Barbie walkie-talkies. That will defeat the purpose of giving her independence, and she'll probably "forget" hers at the Food Court trash bin.

Letting Go

When teens chafe at our control over them, it's their way of trying to wriggle free of our grip. Dressing in odd ways as well as acting in a manner that they know we'll find annoying are some ways in which they make their declarations of independence. One of the best but hardest ways to counter such behavior is by not countering it at all, that is, by letting go.

Blythe J. recalls her daughter's embarrassing adolescent behavior as being all part of a role she played. Her 20/20 hindsight (Rory is now an adult) has revealed to her that "she must have wanted me very much to let go and accept her as she decided to present herself to the world—wild outfits, odd attitudes—and to stop hoping she would make herself look and act 'normal.' Because when I relaxed about all that and decided to stop caring, she dropped that role."

A Flash of Brilliance

At times, your teen might just pleasantly surprise you when you're in public. Every now and then, forget about all your quibbles with her behavior or how she has all her clothes strewn across her room and try to see her from someone else's perspective. Chances are good that there's something about her that you take for granted, something an unfamiliar eye would perceive as amazing or wonderful.

On a winter morning when my son was six, he fell out of his bed, his top teeth ripping through his lower lip. My daughter and I rushed him to the pediatrician for stitches. Now, I'm a pretty good mom, but there's one thing that I just can't handle: seeing my child writhe and scream in pain as a needle full of Novocain is inserted into his gums. I tried my hardest to be my son's pillar of strength, the reassuring hand for him to squeeze—but I stupidly looked up and saw the injection. I started to feel woozy. I turned to my daughter (twelve at the time) and whispered, "Can you take over? I'm about to faint."

Without another word, she swooped right in, comforting her little brother through his ordeal and making no mention of how Mommy flaked out and was at that point sitting in a chair with her head between her knees. Later the nurse commented on how wonderful she was and how lucky I was to have such an amazing and caring daughter.

She was right. I do have an amazing daughter, even though her saintliness came to an abrupt end on the ride home. But even when she acts completely impossible, I can't take away from her that she had one flash of brilliance, which was dazzling and warming on that gray winter day.

So let yourself be amazed by your daughter, but when it comes, realize that these bursts of astonishing maturity, like an ephemeral divine light, can vanish immediately while the usual self-absorption and difficulty resume. Still, don't forget her potential and don't expect it to repeat itself often. Just bask in the knowledge that there is someone inside her who is that remarkable, as I think it may just be a sneak preview of who she will ultimately become.

Incidentally, it's important to take her aside and let her know in your most heartfelt way just how great she was and how proud you are of her. But do yourself a favor: Don't end it with, "Oh and by the way, you never hung up your clothes."

Dr. Ava says:

In addition to the task of separating from old emotional ties, which we've been discussing, your daughter faces the equally daunting task of establishing new emotional ties in her life. This means that she must shift her allegiances to her peers, who, by the way, are harder to please and less supportive of all of her foibles than you are. So when she's out in public and exposed to scrutiny, she's pretty nervous, and if you're with her, she has both of you to worry about.

Your daughter's attacks on you and your appearance ("Can't you do something with your hair?" "You know, you have a big butt.") actually reflect her anxieties about her own appearance ("Do I look weird?" "Is that a zit?"). Just as you needed her, when she was a child, to behave well lest she embarrass you, she now needs you to behave well lest you embarrass her. Just as you had standards for public behavior (no tantrums, eat with a fork) so she now has public standards ("Don't smile too much." "Don't touch me in front of people").

If you follow these three basic rules for parental public behavior, you and your daughter will feel much less agitated:

Rule # 1: Encourage lots of company if you need to put in a public appearance with your daughter. Having her close friends around helps your daughter feel more comfortable, dilutes the one-on-one tension between you, and as a bonus, often gives you surprising allies for your point of view.

Rule # 2: If you must appear in public with your daughter, tone "it" down (whatever "it" is—your too-bright smile, your too-loud voice, your too-stupid conversation, etc.). Remember when I spoke about the natural female competition that is a part of adolescent development? Public appearances mark your daughter's debut as a woman, and you need to be behind the curtain while she takes the bows. (This is why having a celebrity mom or dad can be a particular nightmare for a teen. Think how hard it's going to be for Lourdes to escape being known as Madonna's daughter!)

Rule # 3: Open up a respectful discussion with your daughter about her "mortification mine fields" in advance of your public appearances. But keep in mind that you're trying to make room for your daughter's new sensitivities; you're not willingly capitulating to all her irrational expectations. And emphasize that sensitive consideration is a mutual effort. She's got to participate too (for example, by not being openly contemptuous toward you in front of her friends).

7. Behavior at Home— Yours and Hers

Mom, you're embarrassing me, and none of my friends
are even around.

—*my daughter, 13*

Why We're So Annoying

Teens have a way of noticing tiny things about you and then passionately despising them with every fiber of their being. In Chapter Two I related my teenage loathing for the way my mother stood when she did the dishes. I also detested the way she cleared her nose, the shape of her feet, and even her smell— it wasn't unpleasant, it just represented the essence of her.

I asked my daughter what habits of mine drive her crazy, and her list was pretty similar to the one I had had about my mom thirty years before: She can't stand how I scratch my nose or how I smoosh my face with my hand upon waking, but the thing I do that she absolutely abominates is when I refer to my canine teeth as "fangs." I even know one teenage girl who can't tolerate the way her mother chews.

Everything about us annoys them. They hate the way we laugh, the way we swallow, the way we breathe. If we abandoned all our mannerisms that disturb them, we would most likely die, so you're not going to get anywhere trying to please them.

The Great Monkey Wrench

Of course, the reason our girls go from idolizing us to vilifying us in thirty seconds flat is teen separation, the Great Monkey Wrench that gets thrown in the middle of our idyllic relationships with our young daughters. They need to say good-bye to us eventually, so their instincts as well as their pituitary glands are giving them an early warning that they had better get started preparing for the move.

They begin to find us unbearable to be around so that it will seem as though it's a relief when they are no longer around us—it's easier to leave when you're the one who wants to do the leaving and you've decided that you won't be missing much when you're gone. After all, how could any reasonable person expect to miss someone who is so odious that her nostrils flare when she's inhaling?

The impulse to separate is so powerful that it makes our loving kids turn on us. Since our teens see us simply as nameless, faceless targets—something to feast upon—there is absolutely no reason we should let their snotty teen attitude get under our skin. Your feelings toward your adolescent's behavior at home should not be very different from your feelings toward her public behavior. In other words, again: *Take nothing personally.*

Just Do It

Altering your behavior—public or private—just to please your kid is counterproductive to being a strong and in-charge parent. By doing so, you're not being "nice"; you're essentially showing that you are afraid of your own child. This has even more resonance in the area of behavior at home. Whereas I advocate moderation as the guiding force in determining your own public behavior, I maintain that once you're inside your own house, you can do whatever you want as long as it can't be interpreted as corrupting a minor (cooking in nothing but spiked heels is a hobby best indulged while the kids are at their grandparents').

I have been known to sing madrigals and Irish folk tunes (the latter complete with bouncy faux-Irish step-dancing—my own *Riverdance!* right in the privacy of my kitchen), garden in a pith helmet and not care if I get dirt all over my face, and do a ridiculous dance (ballet, tap, jazz, you name it, although I'm sure you wouldn't recognize it) for the sole amusement of the family dog. I'm not sure of the dog's reaction, but I do know that my daughter absolutely hates all of it.

Teen Judgment

As a matter of fact, this terpsichorean practice of mine is right up there at the peak of her top ten list of Most Despised Idiotic Things My Mother Does. When I asked her about the list and why my silly spontaneous hoofing perturbed her so much, she noticeably shivered and explained with not a little dread in her voice, "It makes me think that maybe I'll be like that someday." Isn't that sentiment reserved for when a younger person beholds some old codger of a relative whose extremely advanced age has rendered her vegetal?

The quote that starts this chapter ("Mom, you're embarrassing me, and none of my friends are even around") in fact was an observation that she made in response to my serenading the dog with my own canine rendition of the Abba hit "Dancing Queen" while doing the accompanying disco moves. My daughter delivered her judgment and left; my seven-year-old stayed and enjoyed my performance immensely. Now, I would never dream of doing anything so dorky in a place where anyone outside of the family could spot me, but inside my house, I can be the Über-Dork who refuses to yield to the adolescent whim du jour.

Besides the fact that doing whatever you want at home is relaxing as well as your God-given right as an adult in your own house, it also sends a subliminal message to your youngster. You're essentially showing her that you are your own person—confident, self-assured, and standing strong against any onslaught of criticism. You are a steady and sturdy oak not about to be swayed by the gale of what other people think, including her. I like to believe that maybe, just maybe, that sense of pride in individuality might just seep into her brain and give her the courage at some point to say no (to drugs, early sex, cigarettes, etc.) in the face of criticism from her peers. Don't bemoan the lack of good role models for your daughter—be one yourself, but for God's sake, don't tell her you are. If you're subtle enough about it, she won't even realize what's happening.

The Teen at Home

For many people, just hearing the words "I have a teenager at home" is cause for great torrents of sympathy. One of the more challenged Uncool Moms I spoke with, Michelle V., who has a daughter, Heather (now fifteen), was chatting with "this adorable older Italian lady" at the market. "As soon as she found out I had a thirteen-year-old girl, she started making the sign of the cross, started saying a prayer in Italian. It was like she was blessing me and saying a special prayer for me to make it through the next few years. It was hilarious, but it made me realize that how Heather was acting—her moodiness and difficulty—was normal because that woman had been through it. She had seen it all."

So why did this caring older woman feel compelled to bless Michelle? Obviously, to help protect her from the demonic possession that teenage girls seem to undergo right around their twelfth or thirteenth birthdays. For many girls, that's when the moodiness kicks in, which is quickly followed by the other two Musketeers of adolescence: narcissism and snottiness.

These three traits of the teen girl seem to develop in even the most poised and polite-seeming girls. Michelle is no stranger to the difficulty of adolescence and often attends lectures to learn more about dealing with Heather. She recalls, "A speaker once said that teenagers, because they act so mentally unstable, if they were at any other stage in their lives—adult, middle age, elderly—they would be institutionalized because of their erratic, obscene, obnoxious behavior and their mood swings."

This bizarre teen personality that erupts like a canker sore almost overnight is so universal that I think Anonymous should come out of retirement to update the rhyme "What Are Little Girls Made Of?"—you know, sugar and spice and everything nice? The revised version would read:

> *What are big girls made of?*
> *Ego and mood and teen attitude;*
> *That's what big girls are made of.*

Moodiness

If you've got a teenage girl, you've surely experienced the moodiness. We already know about adolescent mood swings, but that's not the only form it takes. Often it results in the precise sort of intolerance of Mom's little habits that maybe two days ago didn't bother her at all. As for my daughter, sometimes she finds the things I do innocuous; sometimes she finds them insufferable—it all depends on which way her mood wind seems to be blowing at that moment.

As former teenage girls, we all understand the mood swings and have experienced similar hormonal upheavals (and may still), but that doesn't mean that we are always completely prepared to handle these adolescent episodes. The Clueless Mom might freak out and believe that her otherwise completely happy child is really going to kill herself the first time she utters, "I wish I was dead!" Or worse, she might belittle her daughter's emotions by telling her, "It's nothing. You'll see." Or even worse still, correct her grammar: "Sweetie, it's 'I wish I *were* dead.' The act of 'wishing' puts the sentence in the subjunctive mood." (Now *that's* a Clueless Mom.) And the Best Bud Mom is more likely to make the mistake of indulging her daughter by taking her doom and gloom too seriously, thereby legitimizing any despair the inexperienced child may have.

The Uncool Mom should have a wait, watch, and listen policy. If your angel comes home believing that her world is coming to an end, the first thing to do is wait and watch. Has she displayed this kind of flair for the dramatic before? If her behavior is part of a discernible pattern, then just relax. If it isn't, encourage her to talk about what's bothering her and her feelings; her morbid declarations might just be an overstatement or a way to get your attention. Even if such histrionics are typical for your kid, you can help by getting her to talk, which can help deflate any situation that she's blown out of proportion. Sometimes it works, and sometimes teens just want to wallow in self-pity. I've found that first listening, then expressing sympathy for her circumstances, and finally just leaving her alone to get it all out of her system is the best technique.

> If your daughter is always deeply sad and seldom has the ups of a typical teen mood swing, consult your doctor—she might have a problem with depression that should be treated promptly. Your doctor can refer you to the right professional.

Narcissism

Adolescence is the prime time for humans to become completely immersed in narcissism. Teens will often start sentences with the word *I* and end them with *me* with several good *my's*, *mine's*, and *myself's* sprinkled throughout. Any family decision will be deemed important only by how and how much it affects her. To the teenage mind, having to go to a sibling's graduation is unnecessary as well as a colossal waste of her precious time that could be more wisely spent on the phone, in front of a TV, or with her computer. However, it is absolutely imperative that the entire family drops what they're doing to listen to a blow-by-blow description of that afternoon's scarcely amusing incident on the bus that involves people no one else knows.

Why is the average teen like this? Perhaps it's not so much that she thinks she's the only person in the world, but that she thinks she's the only person in the world in this much misery (what with her crummy parents, horrible siblings, and evil enemies at school), which entitles her to all sorts of perks and attention. Or maybe it's because the adolescent has just recently become acutely aware of her selfness: that she is an individual and not an extension of the family. This is when children become self-conscious and mindful of every move they make, and to them it seems as though everyone else is aware of it too.

They are becoming new people with new identities, and that requires an awful lot of attention on the self to get it just right. People who have just bought a house and are completely furnishing it from scratch can also be boringly preoccupied with their new home. The teen is no different. Her new self is her new home, and it's going to take several years to get it all together.

Center of the Universe

Even so, few teen habits can be as exasperating as this constant laserlike focus on themselves. A particularly maddening result of adolescent egocentrism is their inability to have any sense of time or urgency, especially when they are engrossed in burnishing their personal appearance. Uncool Mom Suzanne A. has to wrangle with this form of narcissism with her daughter Brittany on a regular basis. "Two days a week she has ice skating classes. She has plenty of time to get ready, but is she ever on time? No, she's futzing around, brushing her hair, whatever—so now I'm going to be late picking up her sister. She does not have any sense that anything else is important besides her needs. Even her jeans needing to be washed come before everything else."

So what does Uncool Suzanne do about this? "I tell her to wake up. Sometimes I have to get tough: 'You are not the only one in this world who has needs. There are other people in this family needing things, Brittany. I cannot stop the earth because your favorite jeans are dirty. You want them? You wash them.'"

J'accuse!

I find the corollary to this self-centeredness is that often when things go wrong for my daughter (and of course they go wrong worse and more often for a teen than for anyone else in the whole world), it is usually somehow my fault. When her computer froze at the beginning of a ten-day vacation, she expected everyone's life to freeze as well. Because I am not a computer technician who could fix it, it somehow became my fault. I wanted to say, "When I was a kid, when we wanted to write, we had to use these things called pens, and we had to walk fifteen miles in the snow to get them!" But instead, being at the end of my rope due to her infuriating self-centeredness and the inevitable accusations of my mysterious culpability of all things bad, I unwisely yelled at her. It erupted into a fight ending with me sending her to her room.

Dismissing the Charges

The most effective way to deal with the wild allegations that sometimes accompany teen narcissism is a method that I came upon after the dust settled from the computer freeze incident. The worst thing to do, a Clueless response, is to engage your adolescent accuser on the specifics of the problem. Arguing that something isn't your fault is an approach that will likely devolve into a "Is not; is too" Ping-Pong match. And just dropping what you're doing to fix the problem sends her the message that she is, in fact, the center of the universe.

If the Uncool Mom comes at the dispute from a more adult perspective (our prerogative, by the way), she can keep it from spinning out of control while trying to bring her teen's conduct up to a more mature level. After my daughter retreated to her room and I had time to think, I came to her and said, "I know you're disappointed, but I'm not going to discuss this if you continue to act as if I had purposely frozen your computer. Now if you want to talk about the problem in a constructive manner, then we can figure out what the options are and decide a course of action that you'll be happier with."

The funny thing is that she responded! We were then able to discuss the situation calmly, and she allowed me to comfort her about the loss of some of her computer documents as well as give her advice about the miracle of floppy disks.

Snottiness

The third teen trait that we all have to put up with is snottiness—disrespectful back-talk, baiting, bucking, testing, and general ill temper. Tracy G., Uncool Mom of Melissa, sixteen, finds this trait possibly the most demanding: "When Melissa first started with the teen attitude and talking fresh, my husband and I couldn't believe we not only had to deal with this person, but we also had to live with this person and love this person. It's a really big challenge to keep that love unconditional in the face of such disrespect."

It's not only difficult to continue to love unconditionally someone who screams at you and curses at you as if you're the most despicable thing to come down the pike since flossing, it's also extremely tricky trying to determine how much is enough when it comes to a teen's snotty attitude. Some parents may want to squelch it completely (Clueless); others just let the kid do and say whatever she wants because she needs to express herself (Best Bud). I think the answer lies somewhere in between (more Uncool moderation!).

Uncool Mom Wendy S. says very philosophically, "When

these girls mouth off, you can't just shut them up because they're saying something rude because someday they might listen to you and stop talking to you altogether. No matter what it takes, you've got to keep those lines of communication open."

Wendy is right. I think it's safe to say that more kids go astray because they have no communication with their parents, not because they back-talked or even cursed at them. We must give them room so they can separate from us (and as we know, part of that process is thinking that we're idiots and pushing us away), but make them aware of how their language can hurt.

Teen Talk Translation Table #2

What she says	What she means	What you'd like her to say
[Groan]	You are not the boss of me!	You're right, Mommy. Chores are a good way to learn responsibility.
Hello?! I said I need to go to Amy's house *now!*	Don't any of you realize that I'm the center of the universe?	Mom, it's not that important, but when you get a chance, could you please drive me to Amy's?
Stop nagging me!	How dare you talk to me right when I momentarily forgot you existed!	But Mommy, I already cleaned my room before you asked. Come take a look.
You just don't understand!	You are so-o-o old!	Thanks for the advice!
Leave me alone!	Please, God, get me out of here!	Yes, Mom, I will study a lot harder.
Get off my back!	Die, loser!	Thank you for being so concerned for my welfare.
[Door slamming]	Get out of my life!	I'll think about what you said. You may be right.
Whatever!	*@&% you, #§/&}!	Yes, Mommy, right away.

Let them speak their mind to preserve open communication, but draw the line at abuse.

Curses!

"Bitch." Joan D. heard it loud and clear. A card-carrying Uncool Mom, Joan had just punished her thirteen-year-old daughter Chloe. That's when Chloe muttered it: "Bitch"—not loudly, but with conviction. "I was so angry and hurt at the time that I decided not to say anything for the time being."

Joan was glad that even though she was angry, she had the presence of mind to take a step back. Getting some physical as well as emotional distance is key in keeping a cool head and figuring out the right way to proceed. "The distance really helped me deal with it. I had time not only to remember my similar teen behavior, but also to think a little bit about where Chloe is at this point in terms of hormones and rebellion."

Some adolescents seem to get to a point where they have to reject us in a hostile manner. The inevitable cursing at us that ensues is almost a rite of passage as if to say to us, "I'm big enough and strong enough not to be scared of you anymore." And if they're not quite brave enough to verbalize an actual expletive, they may just fall back on the all-purpose secret new curse word for teenagers: *Whatever!*

Power Struggles

A lot of this typically horrendous teen behavior simply comes down to the natural power struggle going on in every house that holds someone between the ages of twelve and twenty. They want to test us to see what their limits are; we want to hold the line. They want to try to take over as much control of their lives as possible; we want to hand it over gradually. Adolescent girls and their mothers can be like two weather systems, a warm front and a cold front, and when the two collide—bang! Thunderstorms.

Denise J.'s daughter, Allison, specializes in one form of power struggle—bucking. "She has oily hair and tends to get dandruff," says Denise. "So I gently suggested a shampoo that would solve the problem, but she kept bucking me. When she gets that resistant, my attitude is, 'Hey—you're on your own.' Often she ends up doing what I suggested in the first place—but I better not mention it. I find if I pull away from the conflict and give her space, she comes around."

Bedtime

To many parents the word *bedtime* sends chills down the spine. Every night when the clock indicates that it's time for the Land of Nod, mothers across the land approach the task of wrangling their teenager into bed the way Humphrey Bogart reluctantly stepped back into the leech-infested shallows to tow the *African Queen* to deeper water. Whether your particular bloodsucker is a parasitic river worm or a teenager, no one relishes walking into a loathsome situation and will do so only when absolutely necessary.

To these teens, bedtime is yet another opportunity to assert their newfound independence. Kids, from the time they can understand the word, have seen bedtime as something that they're too old for—even when they're three. The connotation of childishness is not lost on adolescents, ironically the sleepiest people on earth not residing in cribs. Sharon E. engages in a nightly skirmish to get her sixteen-year-old to bed. "It's very hard to make them go to bed when they're teens. You put them to bed and then they just get up again. Tessa says, 'Are you physically going to force me in the bed?'"

The Uncool Mom, if she gets nowhere in trying to get her kid to bed, will let nature take its course. At some point the sleepyheaded teen will mess up at school or sports or worse—fall asleep before a favorite TV show. The one thing that should be an absolute incontrovertible rule is that car keys are handed over only to those who get their full seven hours of sleep.

Bedtime or Best Time?

Bedtime does not have to be such a dreaded event. In my house it became a lot more pleasant when I realized that it afforded me a wonderful chance to actually communicate with my daughter at a time when she is willing to talk. I don't know if her interest is because she sees a conversation as a way of stretching her bedtime, or if she is genuinely more receptive when she's tired after a long day. It doesn't matter—the results are still the same.

A psychologist once told me that kids are at their most vulnerable when they go to bed and therefore are much more inclined to open up with you. Maybe it's because they fought with you all day and nighttime is truce time. Or maybe it's because they're cozy and snug, and subconsciously they're brought back to the lullaby stage. Whatever the reason, my daughter lets her guard down at this time. In fact, we've had some of our most fruitful and connecting conversations at night. Sure, sometimes she doesn't get as much sleep as she should, but I think it's worth it if we get in a good, solid, warm, and relational tête-à-tête, especially if we cover important topics like sex or drugs or the meaning of life in middle school.

As a matter of fact, whether it's at bedtime or at some other time of day, the most important thing you can do right now with your adolescent is to keep the lines of communication open. It's so important that, I've devoted an "Uncool Hot Topic" to it. Just keep reading.

❧ UNCOOL HOT TOPIC ❧

COMMUNICATION

A Foundation

Of all the features of our behavior at home that I outlined previously, communication is the one that involves both the mother and the daughter together. It is also the most important since it is the cornerstone to building a healthy relationship with your adolescent who is going through a period in her life when she needs to be able to talk about all the confusing things swirling about her. Isn't it better that the person she turns to is you and not some other kid who knows about as much as your daughter but thinks she's a guru, or a boy whose main interest in your daughter may not be in your daughter's best interest?

As we've seen, the teen years are a tremendous power struggle, and as with any battle, negotiation is often the best first choice as it can defuse some potentially volatile situations, such as (internationally speaking) radioactive arms buildup and (adolescently speaking) radioactive-colored makeup. The fighting with parents that seems to go hand-in-hand with teen rebellion is, I believe, inevitable and even helpful in the ultimate goal of separation, but it's still important that a meaningful dialogue takes place in between clashes. Even though she might say that she hates you and acts the same, underneath it all, your adolescent is still a child who needs your guidance and support.

There are many aspects to communication, but I have boiled them down to four: Connecting, Holding your tongue, Adverse criticism, and Tea and sympathy, or **CHAT**.

Connecting

Believe it or not, you can have a connection with your adolescent and still be an Uncool Mom. Uncoolness is not about distance; it is about finding the right way to be close and knowing when to let go. Some older parents have close but healthy relationships with their adult children. Those relationships, because they have been allowed to evolve, are conducted on an adult level; they are not grotesque dolled-up versions of the traditional parent-dependent child bond that existed in the early years. The Uncool philosophy is intended to help moms find the road to an eventual adult relationship with their adult child.

Connecting is not only important and rewarding, but if you're lucky it can be fun too. Having good talks with your daughter is only one way to connect. You can also find common ground, such as an interest you both share, that will put you in the position of just spending time with her and listening to what's on her mind. Or better yet, just goof around together.

Be Prepared

When you've spent a lot of time talking and listening to your kid, you're bound to be more in tune with the particular signals she may send out indicating that she wants to chat. Donna K. is aware of this and is always on point. "Listen to when she's ready to talk because you might not even be paying attention. You might just be thinking, 'I've really got to wash these dishes' and she's saying 'Mom,' and you're just not getting it. Sometimes, nonverbally, we put up a wall, and that's a missed opportunity."

Another missed opportunity happens when your child's approach to a topic of conversation sends you reeling. She might bring up a sensitive or deep topic about growing up in such a cavalier manner that it shocks you into silence. Get a hold of yourself. This is just another example of the crack-the-whip quality of life with an adolescent. Don't let her throw you; recognize it as an opportunity to discuss these issues.

Sit Back and Relax

Another form of communication that helps you connect to your kid is just goofing around with her. Spending time together that has nothing to do with heavy conversations, lectures, or learning experiences can actually be relaxing. Offer to help her with one of her hobbies and take the backseat—let her be the boss this one time. The shift in power is pleasantly surprising to teens and can make for a much less charged atmosphere.

Having dinner together as a family also helps create a certain amount of bonding. Dinnertime provides a great opportunity to have family discussions—just make sure to keep it noncontroversial. No one likes to digest spaghetti while defending her last math grade. Unless you're getting financial kickbacks from Tums, let your cooking create the indigestion, not your choice of conversation.

In our house the dinner table banter runs to the ridiculous. Running jokes are usually the main course, and everyone, including our seven-year-old, gets involved. My family's style may not appeal to everybody, but it's highly effective in getting everyone to relax and have a good time *together*. Take some time to figure out something stress-free that your family could do at dinner, and then just have fun.

Common Ground

There are other ways to discover common ground with your teen. Humor and jokes are very effective because you can make an emotional contact with each other that's not embarrassing (as long as you keep it in private—don't try the same jokes with her when you're at the mall). My daughter and I, for example, have our own private jokes about our dog. She may detest how I dance with the dog, but she always enjoys making fun of the dog's dopey expressions and the silly things she does with her paws.

Another benefit of having the dog is that she affords my daughter and me a chance to do other things together—taking care of her. Not every task around the house should be seen as an opportunity for your kids to prove their responsibility or earn allowance. Sometimes if you do these little jobs with your daughter, it will not only be easier to get her to do them, but also it may provide the two of you with a point of convergence where you can get along and work together.

All Good Things Come to an End

Just because you made a connection with your teen doesn't mean that everything's going to remain rosy for a long time. While I was saying goodnight to my daughter about an hour after having a good laugh together about something stupid we saw on TV, she attacked me—out of the blue—with accusations regarding my cosmic responsibility for her lack of popularity. Much like her narcissistic accusation that somehow I was responsible for her computer freezing up, this finger-pointing made very little sense.

After recovering from the barrage of accusations, I realized while that I may not be to blame for the popularity issue, I was partly to blame for her erratic emotions that night. Having so much fun had reminded her of what she will be leaving behind when she makes that final break from me.

Uncool Do's and Don'ts

How does a woman stay true to her Uncool principles by not being a pal in order for her daughter to separate more easily, but still have fun with her kid? Like everything else in raising a teen, it's a pretty murky and changeable area, but I hold to this: Never, ever reject an overture for fun made by your daughter. Participate, but don't cross over into girlfriend territory. Let her initiate the merriment, and let her end it as soon as she wants to. And whatever you do, don't pout if she's ended it sooner than you wanted. Weepiness, bittersweet memories of when she was younger and never grew tired of you—these are all dressed-up Clueless Mom hooks, snares, and traps to make your kid feel that her growing up hurts you. And that is a major no-no in the Uncool canon.

A similar caveat should be heeded when it comes to the friendly chats you have with your kid. Obviously, if the conversation is centered on an important topic (sex, drugs, bullies, etc.), it's your job to listen carefully and try to ask well-composed questions (i.e., not the third degree) to help her solve her problem. But when the conversation runs along the lines of a blow-by-blow description about the dopey things some kids did in the cafeteria, or the ins and outs of some gossip, it is time to listen and to look as attentive as is humanly possible. Try to refrain from letting your tongue hang out in sheer ennui, and do your best not to drown in your own saliva. If you find these sagas actually interesting, then you have to be very careful.

Mothers who enjoy teen chatter must remember that these "fun" stories of middle school or high school life are not anything that you need to get to the bottom of. Getting down and dirty and into the nitty-gritty about who said what to whom is not only the first subject covered in Best Bud 101, but it also can suggest that you *need* to know exactly what Tiffany said to Kelly after Zach told Matt she was flirting with Nicole's ex-boyfriend Jason. Do you really need to know? At no point should a kid feel responsible for her mother's entertainment. You should have a life (and if you don't, get crackin'), and it's important that she knows that you do.

Making a strong connection with your teen is a complex area, that many of us—Uncool or otherwise—could use some help with. Our "resident" psychologist, Dr. Ava L. Siegler, has written an excellent book, *The Essential Guide to the New Adolescence,* which is full of intelligent, practical, and valuable advice, especially regarding the topic of communicating with your teen. I highly recommend it because it shows you point by point how to have constructive conversations that will benefit both you and your child.

Holding Your Tongue

There comes a time in any mother–daughter relationship when it's best for the mom to just shut her trap. For instance, I've found that there are stories of my daughter's cute antics when she was little that I am prohibited from mentioning, and I'm forbidden to use the word *cranky* to describe her cranky moods. But as girls get older, keeping quiet becomes harder to do.

Periodically, as your adolescent tries to establish her own

identity apart from yours, she may start to embrace ideas or views that you find anathema. The Uncool Mom should not respond to this by arguing with her, pointing out the error of her logic, or shutting her down. Unfortunately, it's best during these periods just to muzzle yourself.

Why is clamming up a good move? Says Pam W., mother of a rebellious teen, "A lot of times I think they're just baiting you. They want to make you insane. I once read in a book that if your daughter comes home saying, 'I'm dating this great guy named Scar—he's a senior and he never goes to class' and all these other horrible things, when she brings him home, you have to say, 'Welcome, Scar! Oh, he seems like a lovely young man.' Because if you don't, your little honey bun will run right into Scar's tattooed arms. But if you welcome him, then she'll start to see on her own that he's a creep because, deep down, they really are still like us."

Silence Not So Golden

So you've spent a few years now wishing that your constantly chattering and complaining magpie of a daughter would just give her jaw muscles a holiday, and now that she's sixteen, she finally has. Panic fills your brain—why is she so quiet? Why isn't she talking to me? When this happens, it can be quite disconcerting and not the respite you thought it would be. Again, if her withdrawal is complete and very dark, consult a professional, but most girls who stop chatting are just going through a normal phase.

For many adolescents, the silence can be selective—they'll still talk about how they'd be happier with three holes in each ear, but as their separation from you gets more complete, they may stop talking about those very things that you want to talk about: sex, drugs, weathering emotional crises—the eight-hundred-pound gorillas of teen issues. Several Uncool moms I spoke to have had this exact experience once their daughters hit fifteen or sixteen. Their solution? Don't cry or fret—just find another way to communicate.

Shelley N. has always talked to her daughter a lot about everything, but when her daughter turned fifteen, she got a bit more reluctant to engage in these heart-to-hearts. Shelley has since found books to be a lifesaver. "Now when she doesn't want to discuss drugs or sex, I just buy a book that I think is good and throw it in her room. She'll yell, 'I don't need that!' but later I'll look in and she'll be reading the books—poring over them."

Adverse Criticism

The problem with adverse criticism is pretty obvious. Much the way we should bite our tongues when our daughters go out on a rebellious limb, so should we also keep our pie holes shut when the chance to criticize comes rolling along. Kids make mistakes—some more than others, and we have to understand that their mistakes are learning experiences for them. It's much easier for teens to accept their mistakes as such and actually try to learn from them if they don't have some carping critic at home reminding them of everything they do wrong.

If you do have a tendency to criticize, think about why. Maybe your ambitions for your kid do not in any way match up with what she wants to do. If that's the case, let it go. Don't pile on the "If you don't do this or that, you'll never get into Tippy-Top University." Have you asked her if that particular bastion of higher learning is where she really wants to go? Or is it your dream? Many people have ended up happy and productive without an Ivy League degree, but I know a lot who are miserable because they succumbed to their parents' disapproval and abandoned the life course that they actually wanted to pursue.

Be a sanctuary for your child. If she's doing things wrong, try to find out why in as nonjudgmental a way as possible and then together take a look at what she wants out of life and what she can do to get there. Constant criticism will never result in your teen doing exactly what you want, but it will result in a kid who wants to get the hell away from you as soon as possible and who probably will love doing whatever it is that you find so objectionable.

Your Turn in the Hot Seat

Adolescence is a time when kids try to turn the tables on their parents in their struggle for power. Most of the time it's important for us to hold the line and keep those tables right where we want them, but there are some instances when it's okay to let them have their way. In my book, one of those times is the inevitable criticizing of Mom that happens as the young teen begins to feel her oats.

We are not perfect, and if you've done your Uncool job right up to this point, you've gone out of your way to let your daughter know it. Since we do have flaws, it would be intolerably hypocritical to ban any criticism that comes your way. In my house it would be a fool's errand since it comes fast and furious on a daily basis, flowing as regularly as the electricity only with no chance of a blackout. I've had very little choice but to let her go at it. Since I *take nothing personally*, it rarely sticks in my craw, and it allows me to judge her judgments with a fair eye (although I must admit that it bugs me after a while).

Often she will expound on things that I do that she

wishes I would stop. Most are ludicrous requests like, "I hate it when you tell me to go to bed." My answer is simple: "When you begin to put yourself to bed at the proper time, that's when I'll stop." But every now and then she'll hit on something that I do that is in fact wrong or annoying: "I hate it when you sigh loudly when we're talking about my grades—it makes me feel so guilty." She was right. It's a passive-aggressive technique that is preferably left on the trash heap of bad mothering along with proscriptions against wire hangers. If I'm exasperated, I should verbalize it instead of employing coercive methods like sighing.

The most amazing sight is when you can honestly say to your child, "You're right. I should change that. I'll work on it, but let me know if I slip up and do it again." The look on her face will say it all: She'll beam. She may even seem slightly more mature. But most important, she's more likely to respect you because of your fairness and the fact that you obviously respect her enough to hear her out and respond. Just do yourself a favor: Make sure to follow through.

Tea and Sympathy

This is an appropriate title for this section because in my family, commiserating over a cup of tea is a much beloved tradition. It was introduced years ago by my children's English nanny, Polly (all INS agents, please remain seated—she was born in California, and a year later when her family returned to Britain, she went with them—understandably), and has become our foolproof method of comforting anyone who's down in the dumps or upset.

A marvelous woman who has been indispensable in helping me raise my two children, Polly has been providing solace in loose leaf or flow-thru bag form to the entire family for a decade and change, establishing an association between tea and nurturing that my daughter would someday absorb and that I would grow to rely on. Even today, at thirteen, my daughter will send me the signal that she wants some choice comfort time with me by saying, "Mom, can you make me some tea?" As I put the kettle on, we'll start what always turn out to be fruitful conversations.

Not everyone has a real-life Mary Poppins to smooth away the rough edges of life with a spot of Oolong, and if it's too late to initiate a similar comfort ritual, don't despair—all is not lost. Even without the leafy infusion you can still find a way to stop what you're doing, focus on your teen, and slow down.

Comfort and Not So Much Joy

The act of comforting your teen can be fraught with all sorts of pitfalls, the least of which is the tendency for mothers (to paraphrase a recent president) "to feel their pain" a little too intensely. Too many times we experience the ups and downs, victories and defeats, delights and disappointments almost as much as they do. We need to separate too.

I used to dread picking my daughter up from school when she was finding something big out—a student council election result, whether or not her crush asked her out, final exam grades, play auditions, and so on. The anticipation drove me nuts. If the news was good—relief; if bad—I got angry along with her or it brought back feelings of my own inadequacy. The point is that I wasn't there for her as much as I was co-experiencing everything with her. I hated to see her in misery, so I tried to get her off the subject.

Once I realized the folly of trying to protect my teenager from disappointments (I hate to say it, but they really are character-building), I was able to see her setbacks in a completely different light. Now I consider every bit of bad news an opportunity for me to practice what I have always told her: that she doesn't have to be perfect and that I'll love her no matter what. When something disappointing happens, she doesn't want to be cajoled out of it or always use it as a learning experience; all she wants is a hug. With my daughter that usually means more of a verbal or spiritual hug at this point rather than a physical one. But I'm there to support her, and I let her be angry. I don't have to live her life alongside her, but I try to show her by example that you can survive even what appears to be the worst time in your life.

Honesty: A Pretty Good Policy

Our kids are not babies, and they're not idiots. They know when we're patronizing them as if they were infants, and they resent it terribly. I've found that by being honest, you disarm them. It makes them feel that you might just say something that's not a warmed over rendition of what they've heard from their teachers or D.A.R.E. training.

When my daughter was entering seventh grade and had a great many qualms about middle school, I was honest. I didn't say any of that "life is what you make of it" hooey, or any other Pollyanna-ish "up with people" rubbish, I was honest. I told her it was going to be rough—academics get harder, social life becomes more important, and cliques become vicious.

When she first came home miserable because everything about her life at school was horrendous, I didn't resort to the old, "Cheer up!" distortion because I have a crystal clear memory of just how dreadful those years can be. Middle school is one ring of hell that Dante neglected to write about. I told her, "Honey, these next few years are going to be possibly the worst years in your entire life."

My daughter responds well to parental honesty, as I believe all teens do since at this age they already have their feelers out for any sort of lying or hypocrisy. If you can present yourself and your views to them in a completely truthful and direct fashion, you're going to go a long way in preserving the open communication with your kid that most parents find so necessary to get through these difficult adolescent years.

Diary Snooping

In talking to mothers, I found a surprising number who snooped on their daughters—read diaries, checked e-mail, instant messages, and so on, without their child's permission. Many saw it as a "weapon" and a sure-fire way to check up on their tight-lipped teens. It was news to me since I've never had the slightest urge to read my daughter's diary, but then again, she is only thirteen and the least secretive kid I know.

One example of a sleuthing mom is Ellen G., who started reading her daughter's diary to find out what was going on in her life when she started clamming up in ninth grade. "Experts say you should never violate your child's privacy, but thank God I did because that's how I found out Sinead was getting into cars with boys. And then I could say to her, 'Our neighbor Mrs. Whoozit saw you get out of a boy's car,' and she couldn't deny it because she did it. So I got to talk to her about how dangerous it was.

"I read a book by Danielle Steel about her son who committed suicide. He was bipolar, but apparently in his teen years he kept a journal about everything in his life. She never read anything because she was an author and she respected his privacy. When she found them after his death, she said that if she had read them when he was alive, she would have known about his condition sooner. When I read that, I thought, well okay, she's giving me permission to read my kid's diary."

Many moms find out about drug use and sex from reading diaries and e-mails; even so, some mothers won't cross that line. Leila Y. says, "I hated it when my mother read my writings, so I still get riled when I hear about mothers who snoop. I never read Camilla's private stuff. I believe that sort of material can only be misunderstood. I think mothers have given themselves permission to pry since they are worried about something their child may or may not be doing."

I don't believe there is one right answer for everyone. Will I join the ranks of the Mothers of Subterfuge if my daughter stops talking to me and leaves me completely in the dark? I'm not sure. I'll have to cross that bridge when I come to it, although I'm doing whatever I can to keep the lines of communication open so that maybe I can find a detour around that bridge when I come to it. But there are no guarantees with teens. Or moms.

Dr. Ava says:

Don't lose sight of the fact that your daughter's apparent distaste for you and all your little habits continues to serve several important developmental purposes for her. Here's how this works:

- Mobilizing negative feelings toward you helps her to let go of the deep attachment she's had to you for over a decade.

- Adopting the attitudes and standards of her peers lets her develop new ideas and new relationships apart from her family.
- Diminishing and demeaning you helps her feel less intimidated by your power as she begins to develop her own identity.

While rivalry and rejection may be the most prominent aspects of your daughter's public behavior, her old baby needs to be cuddled and comforted may surface in private. Sometimes you'll have the positive pleasures of unexpected hugs and kisses, but often your daughter's wish to be taken care of may be hidden in negative encounters. For example, a teen who doesn't use deodorant and who refuses to buy a bra is saying loud and clear, "I don't want to grow up!" By resisting taking responsibility for herself, she's ensuring that *you* must remain involved in taking care of her.

You can see these old dependency needs surface in many other aspects of family life, such as homework (your daughter provokes your nagging to escape organizing her own work), chores (your daughter refuses to pull her weight in the family, opting instead to lean on you), or curfews (your daughter comes home past her curfew, requiring you to ground her, which then results in her being at home with you as if she were a little kid).

Your job at home is to encourage your daughter's independence in all of the areas where she's resisting growing up. Here are some ways to manage:

Communicate, don't compel. If you have suggestions about shampoos, nutrition, schedules, clothes, and so forth, keep them as *suggestions*. Lay your ideas out on the table, but don't force-feed them to your daughter. (This gives her room to convert your suggestions into her own conclusions.)

Avoid personalizing your ideas ("I think you should ..."). Instead, use a neutral approach ("There was this great new acne stuff at the drugstore"). If you take yourself out of the equation, your daughter won't be able to fight with you.

When you need to get a point across, call in reinforcements from the outside world (the druggist, the movies, the doctor, television, her friends). Because the core struggle is still separating from you, the all-powerful mom (I know you're thinking—what power?), the ideas of others (from whom your daughter does not have to separate) do not have to be so strongly resisted.

8. Privileges, Limits, and Responsibilities

I'm surprised I'm allowed in the family room
without adult supervision.
—*my daughter, 13*

Gimme

When your daughter was little and got a case of the "gimmes," she probably asked for stuff—toys, candy, dry-clean-only lace and sparkle confections that she wanted to wear on play dates. Since you were the one with the wallet, you could decide if she got the "Bay Watch Ditzy Bimbo Board Game" or not.

Although you don't realize it at the time, the constant requests that flow from the mouths of babes are much easier to deal with than the ones you have to field once your kid becomes a teenager. Teens ask for privileges, some of which are intangibles that are more difficult for parents to police (such as curfews) and some of which are related to getting more stuff (such as a private phone line). Because teens are more sophisticated than they were when they were little, they are now able to propose ostensibly sound reasons why they should have what they say they so desperately need. And as tireless as little kids seem, adolescents not only have a bottomless well of energy that they exclusively use to torment parents (they're always "too tired" to do chores or help out), but they also are naturally imbued with a dogged persistence that in adulthood is seen only in stalkers.

Give Me Liberties!

I would venture to say that privileges are at the root of a vast majority of arguments between teenagers and their parents. The teen always thinks she is ready for a new one; the parents are still wondering about the wisdom of granting the last one. Once again a mom might feel as though she is on a never-ending request treadmill—her daughter continually pressing for more privileges followed by her own knee-jerk reaction to say no. The truth is that your daughter probably is not up to some of the privileges she's seeking. But on the other hand, she may well be mature enough and ready for new privileges way before you'll feel comfortable conferring them.

So how does a mother know the right time to dole out the liberties that her daughter claims are her right? Again, the Uncool Mom is groping in the dark, letting her instincts light the way. Different kids are ready for different privileges at different times. The first job is to recognize where your child is in terms of maturity (and by the way, the fact that she may be very smart does not necessarily mean she's mature—don't confuse the two). The second task is to clear your ears of any and all chatter about what the other moms are doing. The third is to provide your child with opportunities to prove herself, and the fourth is to go out of your mind constantly asking yourself if you're doing the right thing.

One of the most difficult aspects of teen privileges is the very nature of them. Each time an adolescent is granted one, she is further inducted into the adult world. A private phone line, freedom to go certain places without a chaperone in tow, a TV in her room, Internet access, an e-mail address, a cell phone, a Palm Pilot, credit cards, a car—these are all the domain of a grown-up club that your teen desperately wants to join. A lot of teens think that getting the privilege is the way to grow up, whereas parents see growing up as the way to get the privilege. And a rebuff from the parent is most likely to elicit from the child, "Don't you trust me?"

Trust—The Ultimate Privilege

When you give someone your trust, it's giving her your faith, which is far more personal and fragile than something you can pick up at The Wiz (well, personal anyway—some electronics can be pretty flimsy). Pure trust can be given only once. If a child betrays your trust, you don't so much revoke it the way you would other privileges; *they* actually lose it. And any trust that is later earned back is a pale version of the original. So it's understandable why many parents are so hesitant just to hand it over on a silver platter. A relationship with your growing child works best when it is based on trust, so you don't want to blithely endanger that trust by allowing your kid to get into a position (such as an unsupervised party) where they are tempted to abuse it.

Right now I trust my daughter with the privileges that she has been accorded. Luckily, our communication is strong enough that at this age I have a pretty good sense of what her values are. When she pushes for a privilege that I don't think she's ready for, and the inevitable cry of "Don't you trust me?" comes out, I say, "I trust you in terms of being a good person, but I don't necessarily trust how mature you are to make the right decisions." She's as annoyed at this response as she would be at any other, but I feel that I'm getting my point across: that any reservations I have about trusting her is about her age and experience, not about her character.

The Baby of the Family

The Clueless Mom has also come up with her own way of dealing with the issue of trust and privileges: It's easy to trust your kid when you don't give her any privileges at all. Unfortunately, it's not the most effective way to develop a child's self-esteem or sense of independence. (Using this technique, Mom might be able to be in total command of her teen resulting in a girl who seems to be the model of good behavior, but from my experience, she's really a ticking time bomb.)

In her subconscious, yet inexorable campaign to stunt her child's emotional growth, Mrs. Clueless oftentimes will focus on privileges as a way to achieve her goals. By severely restricting her teen's privileges, she can continue to control her and her movements as she has done since the girl was an infant. Not allowing certain activities or freedoms prevents her daughter from being able to dip her big toe in the waters of adulthood, and thus delays her journey toward becoming a grown-up.

Nothing to Take Away

In addition to retarding her daughter's independence, Mrs. Clueless sets herself up for a difficult task if her oppressed teen does go wild after all and starts misbehaving like, well, an oppressed teenager gone wild. How do you punish someone who's not allowed to do anything in the first place? What can you hold over her head to keep her in line? I find that one of the best ways to discipline kids is to let them know that whatever it is that they hold dear—be it TV privileges, computer games, permission to go to the movie on Friday—is on the chopping block if they break any family rules.

When my daughter was a wee lass of about three, she went through a phase of thwarting our authority right and left. We sought the advice of a behavior specialist at her preschool who asked us, "What can you withhold as a means of discipline? TV? McDonald's?" I looked at her blankly. We didn't let her do any of those things! In my idiotic first-time parent way, I wanted to raise the perfect child—all whole grains and no corrupting influences like TV. What I didn't realize at the time was that by controlling her environment to the degree that I did, I was allowing her no treats, no pleasures that could be then taken away if necessary. I was heading straight into Cluelessville, and would likely end up as the mayor.

My poor little girl at the age of three had nothing to live for! I loosened my grip on her life and started giving her permission to be a normal kid with normal privileges. Ironically, giving her more indulgences brought her behavior back in line.

Just Say Yes: The Best Bud Motto

Now, it is possible to be too indulgent. A good look at the kids of any affluent suburb should show you that. The number of mothers incapable of saying no to their children seems to be rapidly increasing, and of course, the Best Bud Moms are leading the way, each armed with a MasterCard and half a brain. One girl attended her fifth grade graduation all decked out in, as Reneé C. observed, "a pale blue silk dress and jacket that I had just bought for myself as my good Easter dress! And there she was in my dress and jewelry that must have added up to over $400. This girl was ten—why does she need to dress like this?" The problem for the rest of us is that these overindulgent women are setting the neighborhood bar fairly high, and it takes a gritty Uncool Mom to ignore it.

Even if the mom can ignore it, I guarantee that the daughter won't. Too often the nonindulgent moms are left to pick up the pieces (namely, their daughters' shattered self-confidence) that these spoiled girls leave in their wake after a day of determining who has the expensive, cool, of-the-moment, must-have clothes and accessories and who doesn't.

I live in a town that has both affluent and solidly middle-class neighborhoods. Unfortunately, the affluent families set the tone so that even the parents who aren't so well off provide their kids with all sorts of stuff just trying to keep up. Visit any middle or high school, walk through any mall, and unless you're in a really financially strapped area, you will see teens looking like they're door-to-door electronics salespeople. They've got cell phones, Palm Pilots, beepers—you name it. And then there's what you can't see but that a lot of these kids have (I know because my daughter is always telling me as she extols the virtues of the parents that allow these objects): the phones, TVs, Internet access, and so forth.

The Best Bud lax attitude about privileges can get even more annoying, and more dangerous. These are the mothers who allow their kids to stay out late with little or no curfew, who allow middle- and high-schoolers to attend parties with no parent present, who allow nine-year-olds to go to a busy urban mall on their own, who allow their kids to rent and see any movie they want. When my daughter was six, she came home from a play date telling me all about the video she and her friend had watched: *Scream*.

Working without the Net

My husband and I are in the microscopic minority of parents who don't think that Internet access should be granted to anyone who can scrounge up a birth certificate. Read the paper—there are too many Internet-related abductions, too many weirdos prowling around chat rooms. I see the Internet as a huge worldwide mall where you can get everything from perfume to perverts. I told my daughter: "I will allow you to go unsupervised on the Internet when I feel comfortable letting you go unsupervised—and alone—to the mall" (which is in a city). That actually made sense to her, and she's been very respectful of our wishes. Of course when she needs to do research or wants to e-mail a friend, she can always use my computer, but I check on her regularly.

Another danger of the Internet, while not as serious, is all the porn sites that can appear unintentionally as your little scholar is researching a project. One ten-year-old I know—a lovely girl who is an extremely conscientious student (and the daughter of extremely conscientious parents) and not the type to seek out smut—was doing a report on Ancient Egypt and typed "Ancient Egypt" into her Internet search engine. As she was visiting the sites that were listed, suddenly an Ancient Egyptian–themed porn site popped up. She was horrified, as were her parents—it never occurred to anyone (including myself) that a kid could unearth the red-light district of the cyber world while innocently doing homework.

Even good kids, semisupervised, can inadvertently get into a jam. But totally unsupervised kids are more likely to get into some really unsupervised mischief. The Internet is not, in and of itself (with parental controls in place), a bad thing. The problem comes when kids have too much free time on their hands and easy access to something that connects them to the adult world. This is also why kids who get to hang out in town with no curfew and nothing to do can, with very little trouble, get into loads of trouble. The Puritan who said "idle hands are the devil's workshop" not only had a knack for sound bytes, but also really hit the bull's-eye.

Maybe Not Gen-X, but Gen-X-travagant

So what's going on? Is America just filled with lousy parents, or is something else happening? I believe that our generation's attempt to approach our children as individuals and to have the respect for them that we wish the last generation had for us, although an admirable goal in its purest form, has gone haywire. Much in the same way that our age group (what I call "Boomers and Beyond") overdoes everything—SUVs, McMansions, maxxed-out credit cards, the '90s stock market bubble—we've overdone childcare too.

As with everything else, we've gone too far in respecting kids. They are not our equals; they have neither the wisdom nor the experience that comes with age, and thus should not be granted the rights and privileges that should only be enjoyed by people who have lived long enough to know how to exercise them wisely. There's a sound reason why twelve-year-olds can't vote—no one ever wants to see a Senator Spears.

Treating children as if they are on our level is ultimately very scary for them. Even in their teen years, kids want to know who's in charge. They may like to chafe at the answer to that question: "your parents," but at the end of the day, they are more comfortable than if the answer were: "You are! Good luck on your own!"

In a wolf pack, if a young cub gets out of line and tries to take a privilege that it has not yet been given by the leader, such as feeding with the dominant adults, it may find itself flipped on its back with alpha-male jaws encircling its stubby snout and ready to bite if there's any more funny business.

So how should you respond when your daughter starts to demand privileges that she's not ready for? Flipping her over and placing half her face in your mouth may seem a bit extreme and feral, but you could do the human equivalent: Say, "Your own TV in your room? You've got to be kidding! You can't even keep your own room clean." And don't be influenced by what other moms are doing. I'm sure the leader of the wolf pack couldn't give a fur ball about what the wolves in the packs down the street are doing.

What a Difference Thirty Years Makes

It's a simple axiom to learn: Kids are kids, not little adults. As Joyce R. says of her family structure: "We are not living in a democracy in our house; it's friendly fascism—and I'm comfortable with that." But there are many parents today who are far from comfortable with such an arrangement.

The refusal to establish a hierarchical family structure

often results in a mother turning into a Best Bud who then starts to identify too closely with her child. She gives her child equal voting rights with that of the adults and may allow her—as I've witnessed—to determine how the family will spend their vacation. If the kid can decide where to vacation, then it's only a short skip to the next bone-headed conclusion: that what's good for the mom is good for the daughter.

If a mother has the funds to go out and get herself an eighty-dollar haircut, does that mean that the kid should also get an eighty-dollar haircut (which actually happens in my community)? No! Do these moms feel guilty about spending so much money that they have to normalize it by having everyone get expensive coifs? Or maybe—and this is sadder—these mothers don't know about Supercuts? Ultimately, I think that somehow these women feel that they are giving their kids short shrift because, as one Uncool Mom observes, "these indulgent parents are trying to keep up with the other people, or their perceptions of what the other people are doing." All I know is that my kid's getting her first eighty-dollar haircut when she can plop down her own eighty dollars.

How to Say No

First of all, you have to stay tough. You must try to reach a Zen-like state about what all the other mothers and kids are doing and getting. Use whatever it takes: aromatherapy, meditation, endless reruns of *Kung Fu*—just do it. Once you are capable of tuning out the neighborhood, then you can work on tuning out your kid. Teens not only use examples of much better mothers than you who let their daughters do or get_____ (fill in the blank), but also have a distinct way of hacking at your resolve.

When the issue of driving comes up, a bigger "gimme"

issue follows: "Mom and Dad, I need my own car." For some families, that may be true. The child may need her own car, but does she need a dream car? Forget all the BMWs and Lexuses in the high school parking lot. Don't get caught up in the indulgent parent trap. If you need to get your kid a car, there are many reliable, less expensive ones around—Hondas, Toyotas, Dodges—you'll see those in the school parking lot too. The teachers drive them.

Automatic Pilots

As for driving, who was the brainiac who decided that it was okay to give hormonally spiked, navel-gazing sixteen- and seventeen-year-olds powerful one-and-a-half-ton weapons on wheels to play with? Now I know that some people have very responsible kids who are ready to drive at the state-sanctioned age, but others don't.

The difficulty that these parents face is that sixteen-year-olds (in New York, my state—seventeen-year-olds in some other states) think that a driver's permit is a right, like voting, once they reach that milestone birthday. Does anyone in their driver's ed class bother to remind these impatient imps that driving is, in fact, a *privilege*? Any mom who is strong enough to hold the line on driving surely deserves an Uncool medal because she is definitely going against the societal grain as well as probably suffering through many teen invectives charging that she is the meanest or worst mother in the world. In fact, she might just be the best.

Tracy G. questions the automatic licensing of teens and thinks that she is a better judge, not her state, of when her daughter Melissa is ready to drive. "Why am I the only one who sees that a child who is so irresponsible and out of it that she leaves her hair iron on the couch, plugged in and turned on, should not be allowed to get behind a giant machine and drive on the highway? Am I the only one who realizes that they are going to get distracted by chatting with a friend or when a cool song comes on? It's hard because apparently I am the only neurotic nut who thinks that sixteen is too young to drive."

The Uncool Response

Along with teaching kids responsibility, the old-fashioned notion of teaching a kid about the value of a dollar has fallen by the wayside. It's time that the Uncool Moms of the world bring it back. For most parents, teaching the value of money was just quizzing their kids: "Now, how many quarters are in a dollar?" That's not it. They need to know how many quarters are in the paycheck of the average worker in Somalia, India, Russia, and yes, America—because "average" has nothing to do with the images that these kids are familiar with.

I knew I needed to start the education process about the value of money when my daughter was small and lost a very fancy sweater. She figured that if we couldn't find it, we could just buy a new one. It's hard to explain to a four-year-old that Mommy might have been out of her bean to buy a little girl such an expensive sweater the first time, but there's no way she's going to go back and do it again. I told her how much the sweater cost, and she gave me a blank stare. I realized that she had no idea what a dollar was.

From then on I devised a system to help her grasp the relative expense of different things that she wanted. Much the same way that the European governments, trying to familiarize their people with the new euro, put prices on objects in both the old currency and the new, I would quote prices to my daughter in Barbies—how many Barbies you could buy for that amount of American dollars. So, if she really wanted a new toy or dress, I would convert the dollar price to the Barbie price— "Sweetie, that dress costs sixty-five dollars, or about four Barbies and one and a half Kellys." Her mouth would drop open. "That's expensive," she'd say. And today, as a teen, she's actually pretty aware of not spending too much money—in any denomination.

Needs Vs. Wants

Tracy G.'s teen, Melissa, sixteen, always seems to have something that she wants that she finds more necessary than a four-to-one ratio of nitrogen and oxygen in the atmosphere. All these things, in her mother's opinion, are luxuries. "I try to educate her all the time about the difference between needs and wants because teens always think that they *neeeed* the cell phone and they *neeeed* to be on the Internet very late at night and on the phone." What they really *neeeed* is a good sense of what the word *need* actually means.

To teach that lesson, Deborah K. hit on an Uncool brainstorm: taking all three of her kids to the Lower East Side Tenement Museum in New York City to give them a sense of how fortunate they are. They took a tour of an authentic tenement house, redone to show accurate replicas of the tiny and meager living spaces inhabited by immigrants from the late nineteenth to early twentieth centuries.

Says Deborah, "We went through the apartments—dark, small, no lighting, no running water. I said to my thirteen-year-old, 'Now, Olivia, look at your closet—how many could it sleep? Your bedroom is half the size of the whole apartment.' It really hit home."

Limits

Limits are the laws of the family. If a family tries to exist without limits, the result would be not unlike what would happen if a society tried living without laws—chaos. Granted, chaos in a family, rather than leading to serious consequences for a society, leads to activities more along the lines of kids staying out all night or watching TV so long they lose the ability to control their saliva. For the one or two parents who have to deal with it, however, it's plenty.

Kids are not good with a restriction-free existence, as veteran Uncool Mom Margo R. found out. "When Isabella was a teen, I felt that she needed boundaries with adults in charge in the home. She seemed to appreciate certain restraints and to accept them, but every time I relaxed in that department, things went wrong. In retrospect, I wish I had imposed more limits and been more attentive to them." Take heed, moms of present-day teens!

If you feel that you are the only one in your community to impose restrictions on the privileges your kids want, take heart—there are Uncool Moms out there who are bucking the tide of permissiveness, and like Margo before them, are comfortable in the role of the adult authority figure.

Joyce R. gladly sets limits on all stuff-related privileges and goes one step further: "I feel like my children are underdeprived. Their lives are so privileged to begin with, that frankly a lot of my effort goes into trying to give them a sense of balance. I make sure my kids do some charity work a few times a year to let them know what life is like for others who are not so fortunate."

Limits Chez Moi

As for me, I've mentioned a few of the limits at my house already, such as my prohibition on unsupervised Internet surfing, but what about the others? Since my daughter is not, by her very nature, a grabby person, I luckily don't have the problem with the endless demand for more stuff. But other privileges seem to crop up in our conversations. Keep in mind that what I decide for her now (at age thirteen) will probably change as she gets older.

TV in room: No. It's so easy for a teen to disappear into her room forever as it is; she really doesn't need TV. She also doesn't need a tempting distraction when she's doing a report on The Use of Incredibly Boring Tools in the Impossibly Tedious Iron Age.

Private phone line: Ultimately she might get one (pending maturation), but now what I'm going to do is get a cordless phone in the upstairs hallway. That way when she wants privacy, she is allowed to take it into her room, but—and this is the beauty part—it's not hers. If she abuses the privilege, it's easy to unplug. I'm solving the cell phone problem in a similar way. Most kids I see with cell phones are just chatting their lives away and not paying too much attention to anything else, including oncoming Mack trucks. We have a family (i.e., not hers) cell phone that she has the privilege to use (and we can call her on) when she is out with friends or a boy. Which brings me to . . .

Going out: She can go to the mall with her friends at this age as long as there is a responsible adult on the premises—not with them, but somewhere in the mall and they check in with that adult periodically. As for dating, I outline the specifics in Chapter Fourteen ("Boys"), but generally it involves daytime dating only unless it's a supervised activity, and I encourage her to group-date.

Whither Go the Rites of Passage?

It may seem a very quaint idea here in the twenty-fabulous-first century, but I think that the old rites of passage should never have been abandoned. It used to be that when a teen was growing up, she would receive certain things or privileges when she reached a certain age or other important milestone. A pearl necklace for college graduation, her first silk dress for her first big dance or the first time she attended a wedding, her first floor-length gown for the prom. These rites of passage just don't exist anymore, and I am spearheading a one-woman campaign to reinstate them.

What I really like about rites of passage is not the white cotillion / *Victoria* magazine qualities it suggests, but rather that it enables a mother to grant a privilege with an accompanying message: "Here it is—you earned this privilege, and it's a big deal." Many of the privileges that we give to our kids are special and should be treated as such, but aren't. It should be a special treat to finally be able to go out with your friends, unchaperoned, to the mall. But parents today (many of them Best Buds) just toss privileges at their teens before the kids have a chance to really want them or work for them, thereby diluting the significance of the event and robbing the teens of the feeling that they've graduated to a new level of maturity and reliability.

Too often we, the parents, have also forgotten the difference between a right and a privilege as it pertains to our kids. No child has the *right* to any of the things we've been covering in this chapter. That's why we call them phone *privileges*, TV *privileges*, computer *privileges*, and so on, because privileges may or may not be granted according to the discretion of the authority in charge; rights must be granted per the laws of the country. Voting: a right. Her own Web page: a privilege, regardless of her arguments to the contrary.

How to Say Yes

What we're stupidly squandering by brushing aside the rites of passage is the advantage of having something that our teens want that we can then dangle in front of them. If we dole out privileges according to their responsibility, then we have the means to effect a positive change in their behavior and personal growth. It's a very simple concept: A teen has to prove herself in order to be granted her wish.

The beauty of this Uncool rule is that not only does it get your kid to want to do what you want her to do, but it's also a very easy tenet to follow. Establishing a work–reward system in your house helps teens develop self-esteem. It's better for a teen to know that she has a cell phone, not because her parents are indulgent, but because she has earned it herself. A little pride in accomplishment is never a bad thing.

Out of Sight, Out of Mind

Another surprising side effect to the work–reward paradigm is that it puts a lot of time between the initial desire for something and its ultimate fulfillment. That comes in handy in a few ways—first, by the very nature of the passage of time, she gets a little older and a little more mature; second, she's more apt to appreciate the privilege and respect it if she's had to wait (to a kid, her time is more valuable than your money); and finally, the passage of time can often have a chilling effect on the intensity of the desire for a particular object or privilege—you can find out what it is that they really want and what's a momentary fad.

After several years of my daughter condemning me for not piercing her ears as an infant and badgering me to allow her to get her ears pierced as a youngster, I finally came up with the perfect solution. I told her that my reservations about her getting pierced ears had nothing to do with aesthetics, but everything to do with hygiene. One look at her and her nine-year-old's brand of hygiene and I saw an opportunity.

Still relatively nimble-minded in my fifth decade, I quickly devised a challenge: "When you are capable of keeping yourself clean—that is, showering and washing your hair every day or thereabouts without me so much as mentioning it to you—then you will prove to me that you care enough about cleanliness that I could trust you to keep your ear holes free from infection." It made sense to her, and we shook on the deal.

Cut to a couple of years later. She had really grown up, and at the age of eleven had the hygiene of Felix Unger. I let several months of this new behavior pass so that I knew that it was permanent. By this time she was twelve. I said to her, "Congratulations! You are so conscientious about your hygiene, you have proven that you are ready for pierced ears." I expected a whoop and a holler and her demanding that we get them done that very second. What I heard was: "Doesn't it hurt? I don't think I really want them now." She waited until she was thirteen to get her ears pierced and has been extremely responsible in caring for them.

Privilege Abuse

Oftentimes the natural consequence of privileges is privilege abuse. It's important to remember that as the parent, you hold the reins. Privileges should always be characterized as on-loan and revocable. Follow the lead of the Uncool Moms in this chapter who have absolutely no compunction about rescinding a privilege, even if the offending child had earned it earlier. And turn to the next chapter—it's all about punishment . . .

Dr. Ava says:

We all want to raise kids with good character (one of the final tasks of adolescence), not "spoiled" kids who have a bad case of what's been called "affluenza." But the real character-building that comes from pulling yourself up from poverty can't be replicated in middle-class families. So how can you help your daughter become realistic about responsibilities, respectful of limits, and appreciative of the privileges she has?

First, take stock of your own attitudes and behavior. If you complain that you have nothing to wear, envy your neighbor's pool, or insist on eating only in the fanciest restaurants in town, your daughter is going to want all these things too. This is called "narcissistic entitlement," and as the example of Martha Stewart makes clear, this is *not* a good thing.

Further, while it's normal for teens to be *self-absorbed*, it's not normal for them to become *selfish*. Deciding on privileges, setting limits, and building a sense of responsibility in these years results in a civilized, compassionate, and competent adolescent. The Clueless Mom is going to fall down on this job because her inability to set limits will produce an immature teenager with lots of desires and poor frustration tolerance. The Best Bud Mom, too, compromises her teenager's capacity to build good character because she extends inappropriate privileges that are beyond her daughter's ability to manage.

Here are some ways an Uncool Mom can raise a responsible daughter:

Think about what you want your daughter to learn. Standards are not arbitrary; they reflect your own values. High achievements? Good taste? Sensitivity to others? Manners? What are your priorities?

Think realistically about the privileges and responsibilities that are appropriate for your daughter's age and community. Times have changed, and many things that we would once have considered luxuries have become necessities. For example, in today's more perilous times, a beeper or a cell phone may contribute to your daughter's security. Similarly, driving privileges are high on the list of teen desires in suburban families (and the leading cause of teenage deaths!), while urban teens may focus their fights on curfews and clubs. Your limits can be different from the limits (or lack of them) in other families, but they still need to encompass the realities of your daughter's life.

Take your teen's personality into account before you decide on her privileges, limits, and responsibilities. A bold, risk-taking teen may need more supervision and more limits than a cautious, timid teen. A spendthrift daughter who loves to shop until she drops may need more supervision and more limits than one who's a natural-born penny-pincher. This is not a one-size-fits-all situation.

Finally, say what you mean and mean what you say. Good discipline depends on clearly articulated expectations. ("You may not watch R-rated movies. We don't want you exposed to sex and violence that you're not ready to manage.") If you firmly establish your standards early on, and implement them, you will seldom have to resort to punishment. (But just in case you do, read on!)

9. Punishment and Discipline

What's this new rule—'Don't breathe oxygen'?
—Sarah, 13

An Unpopular By-Product

The unfortunate corollary to privilege is punishment, but those same privileges give you the means by which you can exact a sufficiently onerous punishment. If your teen works hard for a privilege, she's not going to want it revoked. It's a good way to keep her in line—just make sure her life is enjoyable enough so that she won't want to rock the boat. Of course this is no guarantee that she'll never disobey or misbehave; it's just one more stumbling block to put in her way to slow down her progress toward an appearance in the "My Teen Is Out of Control" segment of *Jerry Springer*.

Parents' authority and their ability to punish effectively a teen who's fifteen to eighteen years old doesn't make much sense on the surface. Kids are younger, sprier, and sometimes bigger and stronger, and it seems that once they get to that size, they could easily ignore their aging mater and just do whatever they want, or in some cases, simply pick her up and toss her out a second floor window. But don't, whatever you do, doubt your own hegemony.

So for those of you who have waited until the teen years to try to instill a sense of responsibility in your child, I recommend not living in a house with a second floor. Responsibility is the sort of stuff that has to be attended to very early on, which is why the Uncool philosophy is pertinent for all ages. If you try to be her friend, her pal, her playmate even when she's little, who is going to show her the way to responsible behavior? Better to be the Uncool Mom who can send a little miscreant to her room with one hand, yet can play a mean game of Candy Land with the other.

One of the sappier bromides about parenting is that you only get a few years with your kids—make the most of them (obviously coined by someone who never had to share air space with a teenage girl who failed a test, got grounded, broke up with her boyfriend, and got her period all within the same twenty-four hours). The truth, I maintain, is that we get even less than we thought. You get the early years—before teenage-hood and the rebellion that it brings—to establish a good foundation based on ethics and personal responsibility. After that, they no longer idolize you and listen to you as if you know everything. So you've got to get to it early. Once that foundation is set, it's your best defense because when she's internalized these values, they're always going to be there, guiding her, even if just a little.

The Clueless Paradox

When it comes to punishment, Clueless Moms can surprise you. There are those who mete out far too much punishment in an attempt to control their teens, and then there are those who don't do much punishing at all. The reason is as simple as it is frightening: The nonpunishing Clueless Mom doesn't punish because she has no need to. She has created a Stepford teen who has been so stunted under her domination that the poor thing never even considers the possibility of the thrill of age-appropriate acting out because it will either upset, disappoint, or crush Mommy. So the next time you see a good-as-gold teenager and it makes you weep with envy, just remember that somewhere down the line, she's gonna blow.

As for the super-strict Clueless Mom—the one who admired the Singaporeans for repetitively lacerating a convicted teen graffiti scamp—punishment seems to be their raison d'être. Actually, what really rings their chimes is the notion that they can completely control their teens, and they often achieve their goal through punishment or the threat thereof. Unless you want to thoroughly alienate your child forever, you've got to be fair. Overpunishing can be terribly counterproductive, resulting in a kid who can't trust your judgment and who thinks you're a reincarnation of Stalin.

The Predictable Best Bud

As for Best Buds, I'm sure you've already figured this one out. Yep, not much punishment gets doled out in the Best Bud house, and the reasons are manifold. First, some Best Buds are so chummy with their kids that they let them do whatever they want, including spending most of their time in unsupervised activities, such as hanging out at parent-free parties. With such little monitoring of her teen, how on earth could that Best Bud be even slightly aware of the many transgressions her kid has been accruing? The answer, obviously, is that she couldn't—and I guarantee she isn't. From the stories that my daughter tells me about what goes on with some of these kids in her school, there should be a whole lot more grounding going on.

The second reason is the saddest: In her attempt to keep her daughter loving her and close to her, the Best Bud Mom may often rationalize her teen's bad behavior so that she doesn't have to punish her (oh, no—that might make the girl hate her!). These women abhor the idea of not being accepted and adored by their kids and frequently will resort to the "teens will be teens" excuse as an escape hatch from doing their unpopular parental duty.

And then there is the Best Bud who almost gets it right. She recognizes when her adolescent has gotten out of line, so she plays the part of the authoritarian and threatens all sorts of juicy punishments. The trouble comes when she actually has to follow through and finds all sorts of reasons ("I overreacted; I hate that I'm always yelling at her," etc.) to skip over carrying out the sentence. That's the "all bark and no bite" kind of parent—and as I recall from seeing families like that when I was young, their kids start to ignore them and do whatever they want. The odd thing is that the All-Bark Best Bud often feels that she does, in fact, discipline her child—that somehow the empty threats count, even though her kid essentially gets off scot-free.

There's one thing that all these Best Buds are lacking: consequences.

Consequences

I am an enormous fan of consequences. I love them. Not only the artificial consequences that in some circles are known as punishment, but also natural consequences such as when a teenager insists on wearing her fancy suede boots even though the forecast says rain, and then it rains and the boots get ruined. Instant punishment. Lesson learned. And the mother didn't have to say a word. Indeed, the experience will be most effective if Mom puts a sock in it. The words "I told you so" have a way of erasing all the power of a natural lesson learned, so expunge them from your phrase book immediately despite the temptation to do otherwise.

Unfortunately, the concept of consequences is so vague for some parents that they cannot grab the bull by the horns. I came across a couple like this many years ago when our daughters were in preschool together. They were a nice though feckless couple whom I will call the "Badchilds" because they had a very bad child.

The preschool was in a rather "wheat germ and granola" town of Southern California, and quite frankly it reflected the worst of those values. In fact, the teachers were so touchy-feely that when one boy brought a knife to school, they refused to confiscate it on the grounds that it would hurt his self-esteem (as if the knife couldn't hurt anything).

Night School

Every Wednesday night the school would sponsor parenting seminars that any of us could attend for a small fee on top of the exorbitant fee we paid so that our kids had the privilege to go to school with Knife Boy. They finally held a seminar on consequences, inspired, no doubt, by the fact that their extremely lax policies had turned perfectly sweet tots into obstreperous scofflaws. On that particular Wednesday, Mrs. Badchild was in the audience.

At a school picnic the following weekend, Mrs. Badchild, now a parenting maven, was pontificating on the value of imposing consequences. As she spoke, we watched her demonic sweetheart, Molly, loitering at the edge of a very stagnant and bacteria-oozing pond, sharp stick in hand, poking at a bulbous growth floating on the surface. Periodically during our conversation, Mrs. Badchild would call out to Molly to get away from the water, which the little urchin blithely ignored.

Finally, in the middle of a sentence explaining how much she had learned about discipline from this seminar, she yelled, "Molly Badchild! If you do not get away from that water right this minute, there will be a consequence!" The four-year-old reprobate sneered at her mother, wiped her dirt-stained face on her sleeve, and shuffled a few steps to the right, all the while continuing to poke the growth. Inexplicably satisfied, Mrs. Badchild finished her sentence and continued to praise her effective and favorite child-rearing tool—you guessed it—consequences.

No Pain, No Rein

The point is, if there are parents out there who are too cowed or too muddleheaded to discipline their children when they are small and easy to lift, then they're probably not picking up the reins now that their little rascals are full-sized, unless they recently attended a seminar called "Implementing All the Things You Learned in Other Seminars." Kids, no matter what age, need consequences and the attendant psychological pain they bring, and parents should not be afraid to use them.

Let's face it—our main job as parents is to produce independent, ethical, empathic, and responsible adults—exactly the sort of people who take responsibility for their actions, and exactly the sort of people our society needs. If you withhold from your child all the penalties for her offenses, you not only provide her with a skewed view of the world (one in which she can do wrong with impunity), but you also give her absolutely no reason to stop. Unless they are troubled, the reason kids stop screwing up is because they finally get the message that the consequence that they receive feels worse than their bad behavior feels good.

Natural Consequences

Natural consequences—the consequences that Nature dishes out—are the cherries on the top of the punishment sundae. You can tell a cynical tot over and over not to touch the stove because it's hot, but she won't get the message until Pointer, Tallman, and Thumbkin hit 400-degree metal. Very quickly she learns: Hot = Searing Pain, and you never have to mention it again. If all consequences were this easy, we'd have a very law-abiding population. The problem is that too often God's lightning doesn't strike in a terribly timely fashion, so that scofflaws are encouraged to continue in their pursuit of scofflaw-ry. For those who do not have a highly developed sense of right and wrong (such as adolescents), natural consequences can be quite handy.

One endemic teen peccadillo that drives most mothers insane is the messy closet or room. Forget throwing yesterday's dirty clothes on the floor—that's bush-league. I'm talking about areas that look like an excavation site for the lost cities of

Troy—places where layers of garments can be dated more accurately than rock strata. If you dare plunge your hand into the middle of the accumulated matter, you could easily unearth the jeans that the resident adolescent had just yesterday bemoaned the disappearance of, as well as the Pocahontas vest she wore for her second grade school play.

My daughter, whose neatness quotient is down there with the rest of her teen compatriots, experienced a natural consequence that got her to neaten her room more so than anything I ever said. She once had a male friend over, and as she brought him into her room, she finally saw it with someone else's eyes—specifically, the boy's eyes. Bras were draped on her window seat, chair, and bed. Horrified, she zoomed around, snatching every embarrassing piece of underwear in seconds. From now on, she does the lingerie sweep before anyone comes over. She may not clean up her entire room, but it's a start—and a start I don't have to say anything about.

Letting Others Be the Heavy

Another mother–daughter sore point is lateness to school. Either because of oversleeping, overprimping, or overdressing (and by that I mean dressing over and over again), teenage girls have a tendency to leave for school about the time they should be going to homeroom. The solution, thanks to natural consequences, is easy: Let the school be the heavy. They dish out consequences as often as they do mystery meat and with equal zest.

Claire D., Uncool Mom to a fifteen-year-old, took a while to rely on natural consequences, but she's glad she started. While her daughter is an excellent student, she's remedial when it comes to getting herself up in the morning: "My husband wakes Jillian up, and when he goes downstairs to go to work, she goes back to bed. I always have to hurry her up, and the mornings are miserable. Well, it took me two and a half years to do this, but now I just let her sleep. *I* don't get detention."

Relying on schools to provide natural consequences works for many other things too, especially if the school has a dress code. Instead of arguing about whether she may or may not wear a particular item because it may or may not break the dress code, I let the school decide. It might result in a warning or detention, but whatever happens, the most important thing is that she is learning that she can make the decisions—good or bad—that will affect her life.

The Rescue Game

Don't worry about detentions being on your kid's permanent school record. It's more important for her to learn self-discipline before she enters the adult world. Getting detention for being late for school looks better on a résumé than getting fired for being late for work. When our darling daughters become minions in the workplace, we won't be there to write the fake notes to the boss when they've overslept or to argue with the president of the company that they shouldn't be blamed for not finishing their office reports because their grandmother visited the night before. At least we shouldn't be there—and if you are, you obviously haven't absorbed much that's in this book.

Sometimes the only way kids are going to grow up, rely on themselves, and become responsible is if mothers (and other family members) stop taking their chestnuts out of the fire. If your teen didn't finish her homework because there was a *Spongebob* marathon on, she's got to face the music. At thirteen, my daughter knows very well that I will never back her up on things I don't condone or agree with—and it's made her a lot more responsible, self-sufficient, and more of a self-starter.

Artificial Consequences

If you can't find a natural consequence in sight, then go for the artificial ones. Artificial consequences are essentially the punishment that parents hand out when their kids have gone astray. Since we live in a time that rightly has condemned or at least questioned the use of spanking, our punishment palette has become a bit more limited—verbal rebukes, time-outs, and deprivation of privileges.

The problem that accompanies artificial consequences is that too often the punishment dispensed is chosen in the heat of the moment when the parent is hopping mad, and so ends up seeming to be disconnected from the crime or too severe for the nature of the misdeed. The best artificial consequences mimic natural consequences, but barring that, they must reflect both the subject and the intensity of the offense. For instance, abuse of phone privileges should result in the removal of phone privileges, not in the removal of TV privileges; likewise, a relatively minor infraction such as neglecting a family chore should be dealt with by temporarily increasing her chore load, not by grounding her for a month.

Deprivation of Privileges

The teen years can often prove to be an academic Waterloo for a lot of bright kids, and too much socialization does seem to be at the root of the problem. What complicates matters for the

parent is that in this day and age, there are so many, many out-
lets teens can use to waste inordinate amounts of time chatting
about vapid boys, insipid boy bands, and girls who are more
popular than they are. Not only are there phones and cell
phones, there are now e-mails and instant messaging—the
newest corrosive scourge of the teenage grade point average.

Sick of the amount of time her daughter Alicia was on the
computer chatting with her friends instead of researching
school projects, Sandy L. decided to review her previous decision giving her unlimited Internet access. That's right—just
because you once gave a privilege to a kid does not mean you
don't have the right to review it, limit it, or remove it altogether
if circumstances warrant it.

Says Sandy, "Alicia was always lying about her Internet
use, her grades were suffering, and it caused far too much stress
in the house. So I installed a parental control that gives her one
hour on the Internet every twenty-four-hour period. One hour
to do Internet-related research for school, e-mail her teachers,
and then whatever's left over, she can use to socialize. No more
arguments—the machine makes the decision."

When I later contacted Sandy to find out what things in
the house were broken from any teenage raging about the new
arrangements, she had quite a different story to tell.
"Surprisingly, Alicia just accepted the news of the one-hour
time limit. There was no big fight, which leads me to believe
that under her 'trying to be cool' exterior, I think she was actually relieved. Now she can save face with her friends by blaming
it on her mother while she can quietly withdraw from the typical teenage Internet addiction." Sometimes what starts out as a
punishment ends up being the limit that should have been set
in the first place.

Time-Outs

Not only are time-outs good for an obstreperous adolescent, but they're very good for a frustrated and furious parent. Sending a snotty teen to her room accomplishes four things simultaneously: It shows her who the boss is, it gives her a chance to cool down and contemplate her bad behavior, it helps her extricate herself from compulsively arguing with you while saving face, and it gives you time to think up an appropriate punishment. Oh—and a fifth thing too: If she knows you're coming up with a punishment while she's up in her room, it gives her a chance to get very anxious about what that exactly will entail.

When my daughter misbehaves and I don't have a suitable punishment at the ready, I'll say, "Okay, that's it! I warned you something was going to happen. Now you're going to be punished, and I'm going to take my good old time thinking about it." Then she goes into her room, and I go off to devise an apt disciplinary measure that fits the crime and isn't overkill. When I finally tell her, she's envisioned so many hellish penances that she gladly accepts what I've sentenced her to. In this way, we avoid the seemingly unavoidable bickering and negotiating that happens when a parent tries to lay down the law.

Waiting a while before deciding on a consequence can also help you follow through on your threats. This is true only if once you call the time-out you don't go off and do your nails. Make sure you use those extra minutes to come up with a specific consequence rather than a vague threat or you may find yourself in the position of our old friend Mrs. Badchild. It's very hard to follow through on a threat if it doesn't really exist. Once you do decide on a punishment, make sure you're satisfied with it. It's much easier to carry out the sentence when you feel comfortable about it and are therefore prepared to do it.

Mama Mia

Obviously, you're not disciplining your teen in true Uncool fashion unless you hear phrases coming out of your mouth that your mother used on you (even though you swore you never would). As Andrea M. says, "My daughter will say typical teen things to me and we'll get into fights and she'll run upstairs, slam her door, and I'll yell, 'Stephanie! Get down here!' and I'll think to myself: 'Oh, no. I feel just like my mother now.'

"And then there are the 'mother things' like keeping your room clean, going to bed on time, picking up your clothes, not

---

I Opened my Mouth and . . .
MY MOTHER POPPED OUT!

When our moms said them to us, we cringed so much we *swore* we would never ever say such hateful things to our own kids. But here we are, thirty or so years later, uttering the identical phrases to our teens. Do any of these sound familiar? Maybe Mother *was* always right.

"Get down here right now!"

"Go to your room!"

"I want you to think long and hard about what you did!"

"Because I said so!"

"Don't speak to me that way!"

"[blah, blah, blah], young lady!"

"I don't care what your little friends get to do!"

"You'll thank me one day!"

"When you're a mother you'll understand!"

"How can you live in this mess?!"

"Then what were you doing up there for two hours?!"

"You're going out of the house in that?!"

"How can you be so selfish?!"

"Someday you'll have a daughter and she'll be just like you!"

staying on the phone too long, and I wonder—do I say those things because it's what I'm supposed to be saying? Is it a genetic thing to say 'Clean your room'?"

Choosing Your Battles

I'm sure you heard it during your daughter's toddlerhood from everyone—Dr. Spock, your friends, even your own mother: You must choose your battles. That advice is every bit as pertinent now as it was then. If you try to draw a line in the domestic sand over every little spat or potential spat, you're going to find yourself in a predicament similar to the one Napoleon found himself in as he tried to hold on to Moscow in the snowy depths of a Russian winter. I'm sure at some point, as he tried to fend off the brutal cold by pulling that funny hat over his ears, he said to himself, "Maybe this wasn't such a great idea, *n'est-ce pas?*"

One big advantage of knowing when to draw back and when to pursue a problem is that it can help you choose your battles with your teen, resulting in a relationship that is not 99.9 percent yelling and punishing. Keeping that all-important line of communication open helps a great deal. Too often a misunderstanding, further obfuscated by a lack of communication, can result in a mom drawing conclusions about a daughter's attitude or behavior that may simply not be true.

Bless This Mess

Questioning the importance of a particular rule in the house is another way to choose your battles effectively. Think about what guidelines your kid has to live by and analyze the necessity of each one. You may find that some are indispensable, such as living diurnally, while some are actually somewhat capricious or holdovers from a gentler time, such as keeping a spotless room.

Shari T. relates the advice she received about her daughter's room: "A friend said to me, 'If that's how she wants her room, you need to let it be her space. If she doesn't mind being looked at as the girl with the messiest room in the world, then why do you care?' She's right. I have to let go." If you can let go of certain things that are not actually that important, then you will spend less time yelling, screaming, and punishing.

The Big Talk

Every now and then your sweet little daughter does something monumentally wrong. Of course, as suggested earlier, it's best to let your wildest, most punitive reactions deflate a bit before actually addressing the situation face-to-face with your adolescent perp. But once you figure out what the punishment is going to entail, how do you have that Big Talk?

The most essential point to remember is this: Avoid the lecture. Lectures are to kids what melatonin is to adults. Teens cleverly sleep with their eyes open and can periodically say "Mm-hmm" and "I understand," but they don't mean it. During your well-thought-out diatribe, she's visiting the Teenland that's in her brain: remembering the cute boy from camp, the time the math teacher had gum on his butt—meaningful things like that. She is most definitely not listening to you blather on and on. The conversation may end with her saying, "You're right. I'm so sorry. I'll never do it again," but I want you to know—that response is prerecorded. Teens have some microchip imbedded in their brains, like talking Elmo, and can trigger it to say these obedient things simply by squeezing their own hands or tickling their own tummies.

The only way to get an adolescent to listen is by having a give and take conversation—that's *con* the Latin-derived prefix meaning "together," and *versation* from the Latin meaning "talking like a calm parent and not a raging lunatic." Ask her questions about her problematic behavior; learn why she did what she did; find out what she's thinking, if she feels any remorse. You can then explain things from your perspective. She's more likely to listen when her brain has been engaged. If you refrain from an attack, there's less of a chance that she'll wall up.

Finally, I think it's very important that during the Big Talk she realizes that her bad behavior is not really about disappointing you (although it probably does); it's about disappointing her future self. The problem with relying on her not wanting to disappoint you is that she may be at the point in her separation process where she may be trying to see how far she can go in disappointing you and still get your love. Give her that love, but also give her something else: the knowledge that she's going to have to live with her bad decisions long after you're gone.

What's Love Got to Do with It?

You're not punishing properly unless in the course of it all you fail to hear the words "I hate you!" or a reasonable facsimile thereof. Uncool Moms aren't afraid to be hated because they've never viewed "being constantly loved" as part of their job description. Remember the Uncool motto: *Take nothing person-ally.* Not even your child's most profound hate.

Best Buds often go awry because they can't stand to be hated, but unless you're Justin Timberlake, it's a fool's dream to be loved by a teen. As we know well, children need to separate, and one of the ways they do this is by hating us. "Of course they say they hate you. That is their mantra," says Margo R., an experienced Uncool Mom whose daughter is now an adult. "Being a parent is not the same as being the most popular girl in your high school. You are never going to please the wild animal that you have been assigned to turn into a human being. Forget about being liked. If they detect the slightest wish in you to please them, to submit, then they take over." And you know where that leads you: pleading with your kid to get away from a slimy puddle as she ignores you, poking bacterial ooze with a sharp stick.

So don't be afraid to be hated. Your job is to raise a good person, not to be elected prom queen. At some point in the century, she'll return to loving you, but in the meantime, reduce your expectations about this relationship. It can still be good without being idyllic. Better yet, it could be effective.

Dr. Ava says:

Okay, you've been living by your values, clearly discussing your expectations, and firmly setting limits, but your daughter and her best friend raid your liquor cabinet while you're out at the movies. What now? This is where punishment comes in to teach its important lessons.

Your daughter is not born with cause and effect thinking; it has to be learned, and one of the ways you help her is to make sure she experiences the consequences of her actions. When she was little, just saying no! in a displeased voice was punishment enough for unacceptable behavior (Mommy's anger is a formidable consequence for a three-year-old). But at this age, it's normal for your teen to test and risk your criticism, so in order for your punishment to be effective, you'll need to come up with a consequence for her actions.

Here are some guidelines to help you:

1. Choose a meaningful punishment. For most teens, this will be some sort of social limitation, (being grounded, not being allowed to make or receive phone calls, being forbidden to see the friend with whom she got into trouble, not going to an upcoming party, etc., though favorite TV shows and limits on Internet access can also be effective). The point here is that the consequence must be something your daughter cares about.

2. Make sure the punishment fits the crime. If your punishment is too harsh ("You can never have a friend over when you're alone in the house again"), your daughter will focus her energy on how mean and unfair you are, rather than reflecting on her own behavior. (In addition, overly harsh punishments are not practical. In most families, they are difficult to enforce, and that lack of enforcement undermines your authority.) On the other hand, too lenient a response ("You're too young to drink. Stay away from my liquor cabinet.") is completely ineffectual. The key is to find that middle ground and choose a punishment that will discourage the "crime."

3. Don't drag up your daughter's crime as an excuse for character assassination every time she wants a privilege. If you continue to criticize your daughter for her past misdemeanors ("I don't think you can go skiing. Remember what happened with the liquor cabinet? How could I trust you at a ski resort?"), then being "good" isn't worth it, so you're undermining your own lesson. Remember, even hardened criminals get a chance to pay for their crimes and society forgives them!

While a Clueless Mom might blame the drinking incident on the girlfriend ("My princess must have been under the influence of her friend; she wouldn't drink."), and the Best Bud Mom might think the escapade was cute ("Can you believe I found her trying to make martinis!"), a good Uncool Mom solution to the experiment with drinking might include one or more of the following:

- A discussion about what happened, why, and the potential damage (both psychologically and physically) that alcohol can do to your mind and body, right now and in the future. (Books, videos, and films can help you shape this discussion.)
- A lock on the liquor cabinet (Why court temptation?).
- A specific punishment that drives the lesson home (for example, complete grounding for two weeks – no friends over, no going out, no phone calls).

10. Manipulation

You'd all be happier if you just sent me away
to boarding school.

—Rosie, 14

Learned from Birth

To get the privileges they consider crucial to life and to avoid potential punishment, kids will often resort to manipulation, and from what I see, most of them can play their parents like a custom-made Stradivarius. It all starts in infancy when the teen-to-be, fresh out of the oven and still resembling a prune, learns a very simple lesson: Shriek at the top of your little lungs and you will get food. As she grows a bit older, she learns that jutting out the lower lip in a really pathetic manner is worth at least one cookie and maybe even a Little Mermaid jewelry set.

The more years they accrue, the more sophisticated their techniques become. By the time I was six, I had learned that by trying hard *not* to cry, I could get a lot more—specifically a dog—a dog that neither my father nor my mother really wanted to get at the time and that our house was not prepared for. But I was a wily little monkey, and accordingly, my parents didn't stand a chance—the older I got, the more I honed my craftiness.

You may think that since I was such an accomplished bamboozler, as a mother I would be nobody's fool. In fact, I am my daughter's fool, although I try my hardest to see through her tricks. But it's strange—as sharp and astute as I am when I see other kids manipulating their parents, when I'm in the thick of it, I turn stupid. So now that she's a teenager, I'm striving to be hyperaware of her tendency to finesse me.

The Dirty Dozen

To help me in this pursuit, I have broken down into twelve categories the various manipulation techniques that kids like to use against their parents based on my experience as well as what other mothers have told me. Since children are like snowflakes—no two are alike (and a vast accumulation of them can make life a bit more difficult)—I might not have included every possible strategy known to teenkind. If you think of one not on the list, consider yourself a lot shrewder than the average mom—or maybe your kid is just more devious. Since knowledge is the first line of defense, I present my list of the Dirty Dozen:

#1—*The Guilt Trip*

Guilt is by far the most common form of manipulation in use today, and its popularity seems to skyrocket as the manipulator reaches the teen years (and then again in old age when any offspring try to move out of state). Once in adolescence, our daughters have a better sense of our near fanatical compulsion to do a good job as mothers, and they play that for all they can get.

The Guilt Trip is so widespread that, like a flu virus, it has mutated into numerous versions that make it trickier to diagnose and treat. For instance, there's Love Guilt, in which your daughter might try to convince you that she doesn't think you love her. Phrases such as "You love my brother [or sister or—as I've heard—the dog] more than me!" and "You wish I was a boy" and "You wish I was just like [name of sibling, cousin, daughter of friend, dog]" as well as my daughter's favorite, the straightforward "You hate me!" are all illustrations of this sort.

A related form is the Better Mother charge. We've all heard it; we've all said it: "So-and-so's mother lets her do such-and-such" carrying with it the subliminal message that a mother who truly loves her daughter would do as Mrs. So-and-so and allow her thirteen-year-old daughter to attend a head-banging rock concert in the city, accompanied by no one but one other scrawny thirteen-year-old girl. The Better Mother charge rarely works because it is an extremely crude type of manipulation and one that is all too familiar to us since it was part of our teen repertoire as well.

Another variant, which is a bit more sophisticated than the previous ones, is the Guilt Switcheroo. A multileveled form of manipulation, it sometimes takes a while to realize that it's happening. Blythe J., an Uncool Mom whose daughter is no longer a teen, distinctly remembers this kind of maneuvering. "Rory would say tearfully: 'You're just trying to make me feel guilty!' That took me by surprise the first few times. Then I started saying, 'That's right, you should feel guilty if you haven't done your homework or if you left the kitchen in a mess, etc.'" It's a clever ploy: making your mother feel guilty about her trying to make you feel guilty even though maybe you *should* feel guilty.

One final version of the Guilt Trip is Social Life Guilt.

"I'm ruining my daughter's life"

Cleveland Mother Admits:

Patsy Sucker-Chump of Cleveland, Ohio, says of her daughter, Manipulata: "She says I'm ruining her life by not allowing her to look like everyone else in her school and that her popularity is directly affected by me not giving her every electronic device that comes down the pike. And her future is being negatively impacted by my inability to plunk down $120 plus to buy her designer jewelry. The one thing that's strange is that when I pick her up from school, I see very few seventh-graders who look like what Manipulata describes."

Average 7th Grade Girl

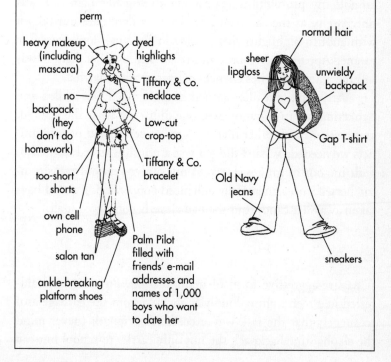

Teen's version

perm

heavy makeup (including mascara)

dyed highlighs

Tiffany & Co. necklace

no backpack (they don't do homework)

Low-cut crop-top

too-short shorts

Tiffany & Co. bracelet

own cell phone

salon tan

Palm Pilot filled with friends' e-mail addresses and names of 1,000 boys who want to date her

ankle-breaking platform shoes

Mom's version

normal hair

sheer lipgloss

unwieldy backpack

Gap T-shirt

Old Navy jeans

sneakers

Using this technique, a teen tries to get her way by insinuating that her mother holds her delicate social life (both current and future) in the palm of her unfeeling hands and that she is cruelly snuffing it out with each parental veto of the next great thing that will promise eternal popularity. You'll recognize it because it is often expressed by such phrases as, "You're ruining my life!" "Admit it—you *want* me to be unpopular!" and "Do you realize that I'm already considered the dorkiest kid in the school?"

One day when I was in a particularly naïve frame of mind, I invited my daughter to go to the market with me to pick up a few things. All right—I bribed her by promising I'd let her get a little candy, but I wanted to spend some time with her away from the demands of the rest of the family. Once she had me in the store, I became her captive as she proceeded to try to get around my prohibition against her dyeing her hair. She was only twelve at the time, and her hair—a dark chestnut brown with auburn highlights that sparkle in the sun—looks just fine to me. Apparently, since I didn't let her dye her hair, I was severely hampering her chances of ever getting married.

Arriving home after a good hour of this, I was addled and hankering for an Advil or two. She didn't get what she wanted, and neither did I, other than the grapes, cereal, and paper products we needed. What I did get was a nonstop screed devised to guilt me out of my resistance to my twelve-year-old transforming herself into a chemically enhanced copper-top. I would have taken away her candy, but she had cleverly consumed it all.

#2—Pity

A passive-aggressive form of manipulation, Pity can be manifested in a teen sighing loudly as she takes out the garbage as if to suggest that the task way exceeds her strength (never mind the elephantine backpack she not only carries to school but can run with when she wants to catch up with her best friend), another teen sighing loudly because the recent breakup with her boyfriend has rendered her incapable of setting the table, and yet another sighing loudly because her homework is just too hard for someone as stupid as she is to do without help.

Sharon E. has been the subject of this last type of manipulation. Her daughter, Tessa, an extremely bright high school student, tries to lighten her academic workload (to make way for more socializing) by weeping to her mom that she can't handle her assignments. "Tessa would come to me late at night and start up with 'I just can't do this!' She'd want me to do her homework." Sharon fell for it enough to sit with Tessa and help her, but then she discovered that Tessa's time-consuming instant-messaging habit was the root of the problem. The jig was up.

#3—The Scare Tactic

The Scare Tactic is very tricky because sometimes it might be difficult to distinguish between a manipulative "Maybe I should just kill myself" and an actual cry for help. As a result, it can be very effective, unless the scheming teen pushes that button too often.

Obviously, you should be on top of your daughter's moods and mental state enough to know when a threat seems real, and if it does, to contact her doctor. But if it's clearly said for effect, it's important to let her know that the Scare Tactic is not fair play. When she was about nine, my daughter briefly stuck her toe in those waters, and I had a frank discussion with her about what it means when she declares any intention to harm herself. I talked to her candidly about mental health, the tragedy of suicide, and how it's not just another tool to get what she wants. It stopped.

#4—Punishment

Kids figure that if they punish you in whatever way they can—withholding love, pouting, giving you the silent treatment, and so on—you won't be able to stand it any longer and you'll break down. It's actually pretty amusing because it readily becomes apparent just how much they overestimate their power over you. Most mothers have heard "I hate you" so much it starts to become white noise they could actually fall asleep to.

Leigh N.'s daughter Sophie's favorite method of expressing her displeasure is sulking. If Mom's going to force her to do something she doesn't want to do, then she's going to embarrass Mom by sulking the whole way. But Leigh, a first-rate Uncool Mom, ignores it and has told Sophie, "I'm not embarrassed by this—you only embarrass yourself."

#5—Public Exposure

Embarrassment works in many ways, and some teens employ the method of Public Exposure to achieve their goal of parental humiliation. Starting up an old argument about privileges that she's not allowed in front of a bunch of people—especially Mom's friends or the moms of her friends—is a classic technique devised to manipulate the mother into relenting, lest she risk public embarrassment. In the teen's mind, once the world knows about her mother's unfair injunctions, there will be widespread outrage and a grassroots movement to oust her.

Battling against what she sees as a suffocating curfew, my friend's daughter decided to bring it up as a topic of conversation when I was having coffee with her mom at their house. Disguised as a lively discussion—a time to debate the pros and cons—it was really an example of Public Exposure at its finest. Unfortunately for the girl, she thought I might be a Cool

Mom, but instead, waving the flag of the Uncool Nation, I agreed with her mother.

#6—*The Technicality*

Sometimes kids can get you on a technicality. What's more, they have an uncanny ability to keep track of absolutely everything you have said to them in their lives and throw it back in your face at the appropriate (or for you, inappropriate) moments. Court reporters should exclusively be teenage girls with a grudge. But that's not where the similarity to the legal profession ends.

A preschool teacher once warned me about my daughter's ability to "lawyer you to death." She does seem to have a lawyer's brain and will use it to trip me up on semantics and inconsistencies, thereby making it nearly impossible to deal with her.

She displayed this ability recently when I expressed my disapproval for the way she was playing a particular computer game that lets you adopt computer-animated puppies, raise them, and breed them. She was hell-bent on creating as many mixed-breed puppies as possible—sort of Dr. Frankenstein meets Barbara Woodhouse—and she used the speed-up feature that makes puppies grow up and breed more rapidly. My daughter the mad scientist got completely obsessed with the instant gratification of turning puppies into dogs and breeding more puppies in a matter of minutes rather than the days it usually takes.

I told her that I no longer wanted her to use the speed-up feature because it was teaching her to expect instant gratification and to become even more impatient. Like some hopeless old-timer, I expounded on the virtues of patience and delayed gratification and told her she should limit the time she spends playing the game.

She responded: "When I play on it regular time, it takes so long for the puppies to grow up—two days—that I end up playing the game for a long time each time I play. And I know how you don't want me spending so much time playing with computer games." Checkmate.

#7—Erosion

Ignoring your negative replies to her requests and continuing to request is a base form of manipulation I call Erosion. Little kids do it all the time, usually inside a Toys "R" Us: "Can I have that? Can I have that? Can I have that?" Teens are slightly more sophisticated, but the technique is essentially the same. They can wear you down faster than an electric sander because that's what they conserve their energy for. While you tire yourself out by working, cooking, cleaning, and providing for them in every way possible, they are saving up all their calories to put toward asking you the same thing over and over again, like some infernal, broken Chatty Cathy doll.

#8—The Diversion

Kids divert your attention (usually attention to something they don't like, such as an admonishment, bedtime, or other limit) using all sorts of means: humor, cuteness, worry, and sucking-up, which could mean flattery (see #10) or appealing to your ego. I remember in high school how we would bring up our teacher's favorite topic, sure that the period would be full of stories, reminiscences, and no work.

My daughter uses the Diversion technique to manipulate her bedtime. Often, as I'm leaving her room after saying goodnight, she'll say something like, "Oh, and by the way, Mom, sometimes I think that up until this point my entire life has been a complete waste." What am I supposed to do? Say, "That's nice, dear. Nighty-night"? I try to keep the ensuing conversation short, but it's hard. She is a master of coming up with the most provocative comments that you just can't walk away from. Was Al Sharpton like this as a kid?

#9—The Exaggeration

This is another classic manipulation—one that we all used at one time or another. It's related to the Better Mother charge in the Guilt Trip category, but I think it can stand on its own. Whenever your daughter starts to protest a decision you've made and begins her appeal with "But everyone else..." then you know that she's employing the Exaggeration.

One of the cruder forms of manipulation, but nonetheless still one of the most widely used, the Exaggeration only works on the moms who are thick enough to believe that their daughters have the time, wherewithal, and stick-to-itiveness to actually canvass the entire school to see if in fact every other kid is allowed to watch fifty-five straight hours of television on the weekends. When an Uncool Mom hears her fourteen-year-old say, "But everyone else's moms let them pierce their belly buttons," she will not get sucked in. She will demand specific statistics before a hole-puncher approaches her child's navel. The answer will result in either the daughter's confession that only one mother has condoned the piercing (she thinks) or the sudden revelation that they live in a neighborhood of gypsies.

#10—Flattery

I've heard of this, but neither of my kids ever uses it on me, and I consider myself deprived. Hearing the dulcet tones of "You're the best mommy and the prettiest mommy and I love you so much, Mommy" might actually turn my head enough to give in on that 500 percent increase in allowance—not because I'm a sucker, but because I'd just like to hear it once. No, my kids think it's more effective to trick me in humiliating rather than complimentary ways.

Not so for Hayley. Her mom, Karen D., told me a story about the unsuccessful attempt Hayley and her friends made to get her dad Al to suspend her grounding so she could go with them to a party. "Hayley said to him, 'All my friends think that you're so handsome and that you look like Robert Redford and you should be in the movies. Maybe could you drive us to the party?' Well, he turned around and said to her, 'Hayley, do you think I give a damn what your little friends say? No, you're still grounded.'"

#11—The Twist-Around

Related to the Technicality, the Twist-Around is perhaps the most sophisticated technique in the bunch. Clever teens who pursue this path know what their parents want them to do, and then get what they want by dressing their wants up in the clothing of the parents' wishes. It leads the parent right to a dead end of logic and, as such, is very difficult to stop or to punish.

Ellie's mother relates the following example of the Twist-Around: "Soon after Ellie got into the elite singing group in her school, she wanted to quit, but I refused because she was having problems staying with anything at the time. So one day she said to me, 'I'm not doing well in Spanish, and the only day my teacher has extra help is Thursday after school, which is singing group, which I'd have to quit. You want me to do well in Spanish, don't you?' So now she's using my words, my expectations for her to get out of the singing group. Well, last

Thursday she came home right after school. I said, 'What happened to extra help?' She said 'Oh, I'm all caught up in Spanish—I didn't have to go today.' She totally stepped all over me. She got what she wanted without having to do what she promised."

#12—The Alternate Dupe

Another classic manipulation from childhood, the Alternate Dupe technique, entails appealing to some other sap to get what you want after Mom said no. For youngsters, that often means Dad, but it can also involve other, more lenient relatives. A time-honored practice, as long as the "other sap" stays sappish, this type of maneuvering can keep the river of indulgence flowing endlessly.

Andrea M. had to fend off her daughter Stephanie's request for a cell phone for several weeks, citing that she thought the girl was too young for one. So who did she turn to? Daddy. "He got her a cell phone for her birthday. Does she use it? No. All that seems to matter is that she maneuvered her way around me and got what she wanted." Andrea's story highlights one very necessary rule that a family should live by: All adults must be on the same page when dealing with a teenager or risk a manipulation frenzy.

Let's say that an adolescent, intent on getting her way, has hit on her entire family and come up empty-handed. What next? The truly persistent fox of a teen will move on to greener pastures—her friends' parents. (It helps if they aren't Uncool.) When Shelley N.'s daughter asked Shelly to drive her back to school to retrieve an oft-forgotten math book, she said, "Paige, no, I'm not going to rescue you anymore. You need to remember important things on your own.' So Paige called her friend Willa and enlisted her to get her mother (who's a Cool Mom) to get the book and then drive it to our house. She had some-how manipulated the situation to make Willa—and Willa's mom—feel sorry for her."

The Lie (Sort of #13)

An ugly stepsister to the previous cavalcade of trickery is the Lie. Not technically a manipulation, teens still use the Lie to extricate themselves from potentially dicey situations with their parents. Bald-faced lies are not artful enough to be included in this chapter; however, the crafty lie is a technique that needs to be explored.

"I noticed one morning when I got up," says Michelle V., "the burglar alarm was off. So I confront my daughter: 'Are you going outside at night after we're sleeping?' 'No, Mommy, no, no I'm not.' I said, 'Heather, I know you're lying because of the alarm.' So she admits it but says that she's going out to write poetry by the moon.

"So I set a trap, figuring she'll try it again the following weekend. After saying goodnight to her, I wait about an hour and then I check the alarm—sure enough, it's off. So I sneak out, and I find she's not outside. I catch her coming in a half hour later. Well, I grounded her and changed my alarm code, which we now call the 'Heather code.' We don't use it anymore as a break-in deterrent. It's to keep Heather in the house."

Fools Rush In

Just knowing the various forms manipulation can take and being aware that your child is capable of all of them goes very far in dealing with the problem. If you think about it, manipu-lation is only a problem if your teen successfully snows you;

otherwise, it's just another annoying habit you have to put up with. The more you are fully prepared for your daughter to try to guilt you out, appeal to your sense of pity, divert you, get you on a technicality, or any variant of the preceding, the fewer times she will fool you. My daughter's victories are definitely associated with the times when I was not on my toes.

Best Buds and Clueless Moms are less likely to have the vigilance that it takes not to be taken in by a cunning teen, and each has her own reasons. The one mistake they share is the belief that their child wouldn't try anything on them. Mrs. Clueless relies on the naïve notion that she is in complete control of her daughter, or what's even more foolish, the inability to believe that her daughter is even capable of making a monkey of her mommy in the first place.

Best Bud's fatal flaw remains constant: By believing that she is her daughter's friend, she would be shocked to learn that her pal would try to deceive her at all. To her, friendships don't work that way, but—bad news for her—parent–child relationships often do, especially in the rebellion years. It is also possible that the Best Bud Mom who is so utterly permissive never comes into contact with manipulation from her daughter. Why would the girl need to? She probably gets whatever she wants anyway.

The Resistance

So how does the Uncool Mom react? Included in the descriptions of the Dirty Dozen are ways in which some of the Uncool Moms handled their particular situations. Other than those, the one piece of advice that kept cropping up was an Uncool dictum: Remove yourself from the conflict. If you don't get sucked in, you'll never be the sucker. Calling your teen on her craftiness, even though she will vigorously deny it, can also work because she'll know you're onto her.

The best method I know of for dealing with the Guilt Trip and Pity is not to get into multiple long, drawn-out discussions about why you don't actually love her siblings more, but to have at the ready a shut-down response that, while validating her feelings, expresses unequivocally your love for her even when she's being a pill (hint, hint). I usually follow that up with: "We've had this conversation before—I'm sorry you feel this way, but you're just going to have to trust me." Add a nice smile, a kiss if she lets you, and then GET OUT! If you stay, she'll try to rope you in all over again. Until they come up with a manipulation-proof suit, this is the best chance I have.

Dr. Ava says:

This chapter has given you a lot of wonderful information in a lighthearted way to help you *recognize* and *resist* the ploys your daughter uses to get what she wants. But unfortunately, there can also be a darker side to manipulation—one that encompasses issues about morality and character. I'm hoping that you are not going to be confronted with these issues, but "be prepared" is a good motto for adolescence, so here are three more serious aspects of manipulation.

1. Kids who *consistently* manipulate others without regard for their feelings or consideration of the consequences are demonstrating that they do not know the difference between right and wrong. Behavior of this sort can be cruel or even criminal, and the manipulative teen can be headed for real trouble—the kind that shows up on *Court*

TV. If your daughter seems heedless and heartless, get professional help now. She's not going to outgrow these tendencies.

2. Your daughter's manipulations (particularly if she relies heavily on evasion, avoidance, and lying) may prevent you from knowing what's really going on in her life. And without this knowledge, how can you evaluate whether your daughter is in trouble? For example, there's a difference between successfully wheedling next week's allowance out of you and stealing your bank card, between lying about test results and lying about attending school, and between buying an unnecessary T-shirt and buying marijuana. Remember the old line, "It's ten o'clock. Do you know where your children are?" In the teen years, you need to add to it, "And do you know what they're doing?"

3. Manipulations that involve self-pity have to be carefully assessed. When most kids say, "I hate myself!" it's just an outburst, a manner of speaking, but for some, self-hatred can descend into depression. Since all adolescents must struggle (some more, some less) with hormonally driven moodiness, overreactivity, and impulsivity, the risk of self-destructive acts, including suicide, is high.

Here are some warning signs that indicate you need to take another look at your daughter's manipulations:

- Persistent and pervasive lying (Most kids lie about some things some of the time, but lying about most things most of the time is a sign of trouble.)
- A pattern of missing money and lost household objects (This is a red alert for drug abuse. As teens become more addicted, they become more desperate for funds.)
- Secretive and/or evasive plans with friends (This proba-

bly means they are friends you wouldn't like. Unfortunately, bad company is particularly perilous in adolescence because of the power of peer relationships.)

- Expressions of hopelessness and helplessness about life, even if your daughter expresses these feelings in a manipulative way that makes you feel it's a bid for attention (A depressed teen can signal her depression by demanding for more and more attention as her ability to cope disintegrates.)

11. Teen Culture

Okay, I admit it—while you were gone
I watched *Real World*.
—Tori, 13

Choppy Waters

There are so many scary influences on a teenager that it can make you hyperventilate just thinking about it, but I would be remiss if I avoided talking about them. So even though writing this chapter is probably going to give me shortness of breath, heart palpitations, and various anxiety-related skin conditions, here goes.

Often, raising a teen is compared to such things as piloting through choppy waters, and for good reason. The task starts out, when they are children, as a fun pleasure trip with only a squall or two to cope with. As they grow older, the journey gets a bit more precarious and the influences that bear upon them become the obstacles that we as parents feel we must steer clear of or weather as best we can. Cultural pressures, such as music, TV, and movies, as well as peer pressures, including undesirable friends, drugs, alcohol, and wild parties that some other parent (usually a Best Bud) decides not to supervise, all contribute to making the teen years so difficult for a parent to manage.

Cultural Influences

Hillary says that it takes a village to raise a child, but in our culture, it takes an out-of-control, profit-obsessed society to screw up a child. The cultural swill that inundates our kids on a daily basis, twisting their impressionable pubescent brains is not what we parents really need, but it's something that, like it or not, we've got to deal with. Best Buds, of course, may actually join in the mind-warping fun. Mrs. Clueless either wrongly or naïvely believes that her child doesn't partake of modern day culture or has her kid essentially under house arrest. There's got to be a middle ground for the Uncool Mom, but what is it?

I believe it can be found in a combination of the limits you set and the knowledge you collect on all your teen's favorite pop culture activities. Like any harmful substance, music, TV, and movies should be controlled, and since you are the one in charge, distributed according to your best judgment.

Parents need to familiarize themselves with the movies, TV shows, and music that's considered "hot" by their kids. That doesn't mean that you have to strut into your daughter's room saying, "Yo, yo, yo, whassup?" while making incomprehensible sideways-pointing gestures and surreptitiously stealing her CD collection so you can peruse the lyrics at a later date. It just means that you have to keep on top of things. Go online to check out the lyrics of her favorite band, watch an episode or two of the TV show she loves, and read movie reviews very carefully. Then and only then can you make an intelligent, well-informed, and responsible decision.

Parental Controls

Some of you may say, "What about if you work and it's impossible to supervise the TV watching before you get home?" Well, it's for people like you that they made parental controls. But parental controls are not the panacea you might be led to believe they are, especially if you have a particularly ingenious and determined child. Consider the story of Julie P.

"When Chelsea was in middle school, she started watching all those crappy TV shows before I got home from work, like *Jerry Springer*. I put a coded lock on the TV so she couldn't get those shows, and she broke the code. Same thing with my computer system and the parental controls, so now I have my computer and TV downstairs so I can supervise her. And I just have to be diligent about changing the codes on both the TV and the computer. It's tough."

Does all this sound time-consuming? Well, it is. At some point in our history someone with a sick sense of humor gave women this insane notion that as children grow up they require less time. Nothing could be further from the truth. Adolescents demand an inordinate amount of time. The truth of the matter is that we, the parents, are the real parental controls—the machines are just our little minions helping us do the dirty work. Parenthood—it's not just an adventure, it's a job.

To Each Her Own

So what happens if you've read, listened to, and watched everything that your daughter loves, and you have come to the conclusion that it's just all garbage? Remember—it may be garbage, but it's her garbage. Everyone is subject to the vagaries of her era; just as you can't choose your parents, you can't choose your coming-of-age culture (if you could, I personally would have looked beyond Donna Summer). It's not your kid's fault that she happened to reach adolescence in these distorted times. And she must be allowed to embrace (at least to some degree) the popular entertainment that makes her generation distinct from any other so that she can have the sense of belonging to something of her own. I'll bet your parents hated your teen culture and thought it would bring about the end of the civilized world too.

So follow your judgment, but if your judgment tells you that every bit of entertainment out there is horrifying, then lighten up a little. Watch some of the shows or listen to some of the music in question with your daughter, and while you're at it, watch and listen to your daughter's reactions. She may be a lot more mature than you think. Use it as an opportunity to discuss whatever is controversial about the program—sex, attitudes toward women, violence—and the issues surrounding each one. As in all things, knowledge is the best defense, and while she's gaining knowledge about the world from your discussions, you're gaining knowledge about the show/music/movie and about your daughter. You can't put her in a bubble—she's going to be exposed to these things eventually. This is an opportune time to give her a good sense of perspective.

A Pitfall

Beware the quicksand that furtively lies in wait for the open-minded mother who watches and listens with her daughter! It is possible that you may actually grow to like some of the entertainment that makes up your kid's teen culture—what then? You don't want your hip musical taste to threaten your status as an Uncool Mom, which hanging out grooving with your teen would do. That's Best Bud behavior, and if ever the spirit moves you, just imagine sitting on your bed in your teen years, your stereo on, and you and your own mom swooning over Cat Stevens together. Quick—think about something else—the nausea passes faster that way.

I maintain that there is a way to enjoy some of the same music and TV as your daughter without suddenly finding yourself buying matching mother/daughter O-Town CDs. My daughter has introduced me to some new sounds that I actually like. Do we groove together? No. However, I can listen to her playing them in her room and not be aggravated. On long car trips I can play some of her music and not want to drive off a cliff.

So you can like some of the same stuff that your daughter likes, as long as you never try to co-opt it. It's hers and should be hers because one way kids separate from us is by having their own culture—a culture that at times their parents don't understand or like. Never threaten that necessary sense of independence by adopting her culture as your own, unless your goal is to become a Best Bud.

A Different Kind of Peer Pressure

There's more danger to Best Buds than just you becoming one. They can actually make your life more difficult in their own little way. Best Buds will try to pressure you into allowing your daughter to do things or go places that are against your better judgment. They will try to make you feel stupid, old-fashioned, geeky—whatever—in their attempt to break down your resolve.

Donna K. had an adult peer pressure experience when a Best Bud in her neighborhood arranged for their ten-year-old daughters to go on a quasi-date outing with some boys at a huge multiplex theater—alone. "At ten, I was still not letting Shannon go to movie theaters alone, and certainly not to these enormous multiplexes, which to me are like a pedophile heaven. And the 'date' aspect also made me very uncomfortable. But I kept getting calls from this mother—very pushy, saying, 'Why can't you let Shannon come?' And when I gave her my reasons, she said, 'That's ridiculous. This is so stupid.' I felt so much pressure that I wanted to scream at her. But I remember saying to myself—if there is this kind of pressure amongst adults, what's it going to be like for the kids?"

The Garden Variety Peer Pressure

Peer pressure. The very mention of it strikes fear in the hearts of millions of mothers and sends the crusading D.A.R.E. officers scurrying for their workbooks and doomsday videos. Why does it worry us so? Because in the words of Uncool Cindy N., "We can tell them things, the school can teach them things, but at some point it's their peers they listen to."

So how do we defend against this gaggle of corrupting youths? Unfortunately, for those of you with teens who have picked up this book because you just now decided to deal with these issues, it's got to start when the child is young. I've mentioned before that one of the best reasons to stay true to yourself and not to change the way you look or act to please anybody else is to teach by example how to say no to peer pressure. Teaching her to stand up for herself and that she as an individual is worth more than she is as part of a group should be a running theme in your lives together.

With that said, what else can we do besides continue in that vein? Not much. Keeping open the lines of communication and thereby talking about the issue helps, but by and large, you've got to (gulp) trust them. What you can't do, which we all fantasize about, is pick their friends.

Now of course if the friends in question are really bad news and clearly into drugs and other dangerous practices, then an intervention is absolutely necessary. But for just the run-of-the-mill undesirable comrades, you kind of have to let it take its course. There's no law that says you shouldn't be vigilant—that's a mother's prerogative, but forbidding a friendship is about as effective as forbidding a romance. The object of their admiration will just grow in stature with your embargo.

Teen Talk Translation Table #3

What she says	What she means
Of course Kim's parents will be at the party.	Kim's parents are bringing in the pizzas and then leaving for the weekend, but they will technically be there for about ten minutes.
Don't worry, Mom, I never watch *Jerry Springer*.	Who needs to when there's *Real World* and Internet porn?
She's a nice girl—and really cool!	She's a freaky girl who's into all sorts of things that you don't approve of—and you'd hate her!
Oh, it's just going to be a few girls getting together and hanging out—just like last time.	Maybe Dan will bring Jeff and I'll get to make out with *him* this time.
It's only rated R for the language and everyone in my school talks like that anyway. Except me.	I hope the %#@& she lets me go—I heard that they have sex in it, and you get to see Ryan Phillipe's ass.
[Upon coming home after she's been out with friends:] I'm so tired, I'm just going right up to bed. Good night!	I'm getting out of here as fast as I can so you don't have a chance to smell my breath or check out my pupils. Good night!

Parent-Free Parties

What could possibly possess a mother to let her teen have a party and then slip away, missing all the "fun"? These women are at the very top of the Best Bud category but obviously pretty low in the IQ category. (Judy L. says, "There are some parents in my town who not only give their kids the house until midnight for parties, but supply the keg of beer.") Not only can kids get into a lot of trouble when left to their own devices—trouble involving drugs, drinking, and sex—but also these unsupervised shindigs can end in tragedy. Deadly fistfights, overdoses, gang rapes—all of these and more are possible and real, as any newspaper can tell you.

Peggy O. related one party to me that her twelve-year-old daughter Nina told her all about. "A bunch of kids in her grade were at this party. I wouldn't let Nina go because it was unsupervised, but afterwards her friends told her some of what had gone on. It was in a very, very large home where there were several computers and nobody was supervising where they were going online—chat rooms, porn sites—who knows? And there were also bedrooms that were being used. And some children were coming out with certain parts of their clothing missing—twelve years old!"

What, as an Uncool Mom, can you do? First of all, always be present when your kid has a party. And if your daughter has been invited to one? It is not out of line to call the parent of the party-giver and question her about the nature of the ensuing fête as well as her whereabouts during it. Unlike much of the Uncool philosophy of moderation that I've laid out, when it comes to unsupervised parties, there is no middle ground.

The Hard Stuff

My purpose in writing this chapter was not to tackle the catastrophic menace of drugs and alcohol. Both of these problems are huge issues that should be handled by someone in the medical field. I'm including a little bit on drinking and drugs to provide some suggestions for preventing a problem from developing, not to solve a preexisting one.

If your child is involved in either drug or alcohol abuse, please contact a professional in the medical or psychiatric field.

Drinking

Just as I think it's important not to demonize alcohol as kids are growing up, it's equally important not to glamorize it. In my house, my husband has chosen not to drink, but I still might have a drink before dinner or wine with my meals. It's no big thing either way. But neither my husband nor I rely on that alone. We discuss with our daughter the ugly side of alcohol and encourage her to hold off until she reaches the legal age. A few years ago, I went to a party, drank on an empty stomach, and inadvertently got smashed. The hellacious hangover I suffered through the next day (Easter of all days, and we were scheduled to go to a fancy brunch—just try bending over to put on panty hose with a raging headache) was probably better than any anti-alcohol abuse lessons I could have dreamed up.

Tina G. came up with an unconventional approach when she and her friend found their sixteen-year-old daughters after the girls had raided the liquor cabinet at a sleepover.

"Erin was passed out but woke up and was sick. Her friend was sick and sitting on the floor. They could barely talk. I took Erin home and helped her get through it, and in the morning we had a long talk about the dangers of alcohol poisoning, etc.—all things I have taught her before. I also gave her a great imitation of what she looked like. Not very pretty. Later my friend and I realized that we should have videotaped their behavior: what they sounded like, what they looked like. We were sure that had we been able to play that tape to them, they would think twice about ever getting in that condition again."

Drugs

Again, I'm not the one to turn to if the specter of drugs has invaded your life. The one piece of advice that I do feel qualified to mention is a suggestion from one of the Uncool Moms, Karen D., on how to discuss drugs with your child.

"I've been discussing drugs with Hayley for a long time. She's thirteen now, but I started much earlier. I told her before she went to middle school, 'By the time you graduate from eighth grade, it is almost undeniable that somebody will approach you with drugs. And it's not going to be the big bad wolf in a black leather jacket with cigarettes in his pocket. It might be somebody you admire or a friend of yours—just the nice girl or the nice boy. And that's going to be the person that it's going to be hard to say no to.' "

So from music to undesirable friends to drugs, as you pilot the choppy waters of adolescence, the best thing you can do is keep the communication going. Talking with your teen can provide you with the map that you sorely need, so both of you can get a glimpse of the obstacles ahead and troubleshoot them any way you can.

Dr. Ava says:

In today's times, when your daughter is exposed to so much so soon, your job of supervising her becomes more important at the same time that it becomes more difficult. But you need to keep negotiating that fine line we've discussed between *overexposure* and *overprotection*. Let's take a look at what you're afraid of in these years, and what you can do about it:

The problem: The earlier onset of puberty in girls (often by eleven to twelve years old) has put a great deal of pressure on your daughter. It's hard to manage the body of a woman with the mind of a child.

The solution: You need to discuss your values and standards with your daughter earlier in your daughter's life (by eight or nine years old) so by the time she reaches adolescence you have already set down a strong foundation for the challenges she'll be facing. In addition, as your daughter grows, you'll need to stand firm about appropriate limits and be capable of enforcing prohibitions. I assure you that despite her protests, she'll be grateful for your interventions.

The problem: Sex is more of a risk and drugs are more widespread and perilous in this generation.

The solution: "Just say no!" doesn't work for sex or drugs or alcohol. Worse, it cuts off vital communication between you and your daughter. To help her keep herself sexually safe, you need to alert her to the teenage epidemic of some pretty bad sexually transmitted diseases. (Don't be afraid to make them sound really yucky—a little fear advances your cause!) Emphasize how important it is *not* to engage in sex until you're really, really ready, emotionally and physically, and point out how much she'll need to know about her partner to feel secure.

To keep your daughter safe from the widespread abuse of drugs and alcohol among teens, underscore that *illegal* drugs are particularly dangerous because they're processed by criminals; she won't know what's been put in it or where it came from. Focus on the *present* risks in her life (decreased ability to concentrate in school, potential for real addiction, breakdown of her immunological system, sudden death, etc.) Remember, teenagers have very little sense of the future.

The problem: The teen years are the *normal* time to experiment with adult behavior and that includes sex, smoking, drugs, and alcohol. (Of course, it also includes holding down a job, becoming financially independent, and caring for others, but this kind of adult behavior doesn't keep you up nights.)

The solution: Recognize that most teens are going to experiment with smoking, drinking, drugs, and sex (one or all of the above). What you're hoping is that the experiment doesn't turn into a threat to your daughter's well-being. Her protection lies back in those childhood years when you taught her to value herself and her body. Now, more than ever, keep talking and keep reinforcing these feelings!

12. School

At school, on the popularity food chain, I'm plankton.
—Bella, 15

A Home Away from Home

Whereas parents may see school either as necessary preparation for kids to grow up and become functioning, taxpaying citizens or as a brilliantly conceived and well-needed six-and-a-half-hour respite for mom, our children see it much differently. Yes, if you ask them point-blank, they'll be more than happy to inform you that for them it is a particularly cruel form of hell (and for some that may be true), but school for the adolescent represents something far more complicated.

As a child separates from her parents, she gradually needs to transfer her emotions, trust, and reliance away from her family and toward a different social structure. That, more often than not, happens to be school. Since she spends such a great amount of the waking day there, it is bound to become, as she grows older, the center of her life. School embodies her present (the social aspects) as well as her future (the academic aspects). Arguments about school arise between parents and kids when kids view their present, rather than their future, as far more important to their happiness, while parents see things in exactly the opposite way. (Why should this area be any different from all the other parts of our lives with our darling adolescents?)

Although we all want our children to do well in school, some parents may have a more intense interest in their kids achieving academic excellence than others do. The issue at hand is how that interest is expressed—from actually gluing and painting her daughter's model of an Iroquois longhouse together herself to strapping a book to her child's face and locking her in her bedroom.

The Eternal Student

We've probably all fallen prey to the desire to have our kids' projects knock the socks off their teachers. We convince ourselves that it's okay with all sorts of clever rationalizations— "She's too young to handle the scissors," "The glue would get all over if she did it," "It really was all her idea; she just told me where to put things"—the list could go on and on. The worst thing a teacher can tell a kid is that it's okay to get a little help from mom. What a mistake—it gives moms carte blanche to construct some impossibly professional atom, diorama, or sugar-cube replica of Stonehenge complete with little licorice Druids. Why do we feel so compelled? Maybe it's because we now finally all possess the fine motor skills to be the best and we can't help ourselves.

What kind of mom is responsible for making schoolwork a joint endeavor? Some are Best Buds, who want to do everything with their daughters, whether it's hanging out or home-work. After all, that's what friends are for. But academic overin-volvement is not the sole domain of the Best Bud. Mrs. Clueless can be equally guilty. Refusing to recognize that her baby is growing up, she thinks that the kid may actually still need Mommy's help, or at least needs to be shown the way so that she will still bring home good grades. The notion of letting her girl stand on her own two feet and earn the good grades herself (or not, as the case may be) is a completely foreign con-cept to her.

The truth is, I don't think you can pin all this on either Best Bud or Clueless. I think that school—at least the academic side of school and the pressures to have your kid succeed—engenders a completely different mom subset, the Execu-Mom.

Execu-Moms

The Execu-Mom is the regional manager of her child's school career and future: She does whatever it takes—child's happiness be damned—to make her kid the best in the school so that she can go to some Ivy League college that might not even be the right choice for her in the first place.

It takes a strong will and determined mind to resist being influenced by the Execu-Moms who might tell you all about Jenny's lessons and Jenny's grades and Jenny's general perfec-tion. It makes you want to get cracking so that your poor kid doesn't get left behind in Super-Jenny's violin-playing, ballet-dancing, straight-A-getting dust. But resist you must. Even par-ticipating a little can bring you closer to the center of the maelstrom, which will pull you into its Execu-Mom depths, never to be heard saying reasonable things about your own child again. It's a slippery slope.

These Execu-Moms tend to be the parents who force their kids to get As at the expense of everything else in their lives. I've heard of one thirteen-year-old girl who gets upset and cries if she gets any grade lower than a 95 percent. What kind of parenting is that? Will this kid be successful? Maybe. Will she be happy? No. A medical professional that I spoke to told me about the surprising number of smart teenagers who are in the local psychiatric hospital after frying their brains with drugs because they couldn't take the pressure of having to get perfect grades and be virtuoso musicians too.

It Can Happen to Anyone

Not everybody who gets too involved in her daughter's homework is going to go the way of the Execu-Mom, but it's important to realize that all of us—Best Buds, Clueless Moms, and Uncool Moms—can all become homework usurpers. Almost everyone is capable and probably culpable of doing the algebra problem that your kid can't do or the research that she won't do. The difficulty in helping your kid do her work comes when she becomes dependent on your input and develops no internal ability to do things on her own, trust her own instincts, or have pride in her own work—no matter how flawed. Obviously, for a teen to complete a successful separation from her mother, she needs all of those.

But don't despair—even if you regularly catch yourself finding the value for x or writing introductory paragraphs about indoor heating techniques during the Roman Empire, you can still be reclaimed. Whenever you feel the urge to appropriate an assignment—STOP. Tell your daughter she can do it herself, or with any luck she'll find a way to tell you.

Ten Ways of Knowing You Are Too Involved
in Your Daughter's Homework

1. When she enters the Science Fair, you're more proud of the project than you are of her.

2. After she hands in a report on Ptolemy, you still do more research about him on the Internet.

3. You're the one who wants to save the Civil War diorama. She wants to throw it away.

4. For the first time in your life you know the difference between a sine and a cosine.

5. Going back to college seems pretty easy.

6. You treat yourself to a Snickers bar when her poem gets an A.

7. You know the Gettysburg Address cold.

8. You get defensive when her teacher gives the Ptolemy report a B-.

9. You have a dream that you're promoted to the next grade.

10. You know all the obscene graffiti in her history book.

Uncool about School

The need for adolescents to take responsibility for their own work is precisely why the Execu-Mom style—either the Do-It-Yourself approach to homework (that is, the mom doing the kid's homework herself) or "The Great Santini" approach of sitting on your kids to make sure they bring home the best grades—is so damaging. For years we've been bombarded with news reports and studies that show that kids who have parents who are involved in their schooling often get better grades. But by being excessively involved in her child's schoolwork, the Execu-Mom prevents her daughter from taking control, and thus responsibility for a part of her life which, when she hits college, will lie completely on her solitary shoulders.

Meredith L., an exemplary Uncool Mom, remembers how she dealt with the school responsibility issue. "During Shana's junior year in high school, I decided to stop battling her about doing her homework. I got her a day-planner and said, 'You're on your own now. Write down your assignments and check them off as you complete them.' A few days passed and Shana said, 'Aren't you going to tell me to do my homework?' I said, 'If you haven't figured out by now what you need to do, what point is there in my telling you?' From then on she became very responsible. It was one of those threshold moments—she visibly became more of an adult and gave up the childish struggle. But I had to give it up first."

The Myth of the Infant Ivy Leaguer

When babies are born, their parents start to develop all sorts of dreams and expectations for them even before their tiny heads harden. Consider Mr. and Mrs. Bo Einstein. Convinced their little princess will be brilliant (how could she not be—her parents are), they put her in tiny Harvard onesies, Yale bibs, and Princeton diaper covers. Her college résumé starts at age two when they enroll her in art enrichment classes, prereading classes, and Suzuki method piano lessons. They expect nothing less than perfection in everything she does because she is, after all, the culmination of their great genes.

WRONG! As we know, children are their own persons, not extensions of their parents. Our ideas of what our daughters may become are only *our* ideas—not theirs. And sometimes a parent is faced with the reality that her kid is not the prodigy that she thought, or not even the really good student that she was when she was younger.

The Uncool Mom tries to take her child as she is—celebrating her talents and abilities while accepting her limitations in a nonjudgmental way. Of course this is much easier to write down than to do. It's sometimes very difficult to realize that your daughter is never going to be who you thought she was for the last fifteen years, but it's imperative that you keep the notion of acceptance front and center in your mind. If you've ever said to your kid, "Just try your hardest," now it's your turn.

A Delicate Balance

Like most Uncool Mom policies, keeping out of your daughter's schoolwork and not pushing her to succeed the way you did or the way you think she should requires a subtle hand. You want your daughter to be happy, and you don't want her to feel that she's not living up to some idealized version of her that's in your mind. On the other hand, as a parent you can't just stand by and watch her flake out and shrink her opportunities simply because she doesn't see herself as an achiever.

When her daughter Lindsay was in middle school (a classic time for previously high-achieving students to slack off), Judy L. says, "I told her that the key to her freedom as an adult is education, and the key to her freedom as a teenager is also education—meaning that if she proved to be a responsible student in school, then I could believe she could be responsible in other areas in her life and therefore give her more privileges."

Later on, Lindsay, a talented pianist, set her heart on a particular college known for its wonderful music program. Says

Judy, "It's not an easy school to get into. You not only have to have talent, but also good grades and a high SAT score. I knew me just telling her wouldn't amount to anything, so we visited the school for a weekend. That was the best move I made. She came back totally motivated and began to take school more seriously."

My Brief Foray into Execu-Mom-ism

My firsthand experience with this problem came last year when my daughter, who has had a strong interest in singing and songwriting for the last three years or so, was presented with an amazing opportunity by her seventh grade music teacher. My daughter had written a patriotic song, which she sang to her class for extra credit. Impressed, the teacher told her that if she transcribed the song into musical notation, the entire chorus would sing it for their upcoming spring concert.

My daughter was proud, and of course I was thrilled. Since she doesn't read music, she had to get help from one of the other teachers to get the song in shape, but for some reason she kept dragging her feet. Finally, I stepped in and offered to set up a time when she could spend an afternoon with a professional songwriter whom I had met through a friend. She balked, but I, infected with Execu-Mom-itis, insisted, until my husband forced me to be reasonable.

When my Execu-Mom squall subsided, I realized that all I wanted was for her to choose two activities and to stick with them. She reminded me that she writes all the time and is very committed to it. We negotiated a settlement that ended up pleasing both of us: She would pursue things that she was enthusiastic about, as long as she stuck with one, and would join one other activity trying to find another interest, with the understanding that once she found one, she would stick with that as well.

Social Aspects

That night she confessed that one reason she didn't want to go through with the song was that she feared some sort of harassment from some of the mean popular girls who were in chorus. That revelation made me sad. School should be an adolescent's haven—a place to safely separate from her parents as well as a place where she can find who she really is. When bullies enter the picture, making school far less of a refuge, the pain and dread that can result can not only keep someone from publicly exploring her potential, but can also make her life miserable.

Just about every adolescent girl experiences an incident in which other, usually more popular, girls get their jollies by inflicting on her cruel and unusual psychological pain. Such taunting, spreading of malicious rumors, mocking with humiliating remarks, pencil throwing (a specialty at my daughter's school), and other forms of teen torture can be bitterly upsetting and infuriating. And not just to you. Yes, your daughter may be hurt by the callous actions of a few entitled little harpies-in-training, but you don't want to compound the pain with your well-meaning protection.

One-Woman Posse

I don't know about you, but when my daughter is tormented by the vicious brutality that only war criminals and middle school girls can comfortably pull off, I seethe. My blood rushes through me with such Mach 5 speed that I feel myself transforming—pupils narrowing to feline slits, fangs growing, ready to pounce on all the snotty, pubescent gorgons in seventy-five-dollar T-shirts I see. Horrid growls emanate from a gut I didn't know I had. And like Scrooge's final spirit, I long to show them the picture of their inevitable future: them, grasping a phone, pitifully begging my more successful daughter to change long-distance companies.

I know that this is as much a mother-tiger reaction as it is the response, long buried, that I wanted to make when I was in junior high and Angela Kirkland tangled numerous spit-glazed sticky candies all through my waist-length hair during social studies class (we were probably studying a unit on tolerance). When adolescent girls grow up to have adolescent girls, they (we) are forced to relive the trauma and the blood-boiling frustration of powerlessness that comes with being popular-girl prey.

Let Me at 'Em

Regardless of which little blighter is responsible for wreaking such havoc on your little girl, the first thing to do is remember that she is no longer a little girl. Unlike when she was a pre-schooler and some nasty little troll of a classmate pushed her down or stole a toy and you could deliver justice with a simple tongue-lashing, that won't fly anymore. You can't treat an adolescent who is trying to grow up like a helpless baby. She has to fight her own battles and learn that after a hurting there's a healing, and that she really can manage it herself.

This is not to say you should completely opt out. Hardly. She needs you in these tense moments. But whereas a Clueless Mom will stomp into the principal's office and demand the head of the offending child (and in doing so, mortifying her own), the Uncool Mom will wait and see, encouraging her daughter to handle things on her own, interceding only if the situation gets out of hand.

Another pitfall that incidentally seems to be right in the path of the Best Bud Mom is reacting to your daughter's social woes as if they were your own. Beware of the problem, discussed earlier, of reliving the misery of your own teen years. I know that my daughter has her own version of Angela Kirkland, but this one is her own nemesis, not mine. No amount of helping her plot revenge on her enemy is going to give Angela her comeuppance, especially since she, in all likelihood, is now a middle-aged law-abiding taxpayer who probably only vaguely remembers me, my hair, or her eighth grade diabolical use of Life Savers.

Although I still wonder what a woman like Angela does if she has mysteriously given birth to an unpopular kid and little Lame-o comes home complaining of popular girl harassment: "They did what? Well, I really don't know what to do. You see, Sweetie, when Mommy was your age, Mommy used to be the popular bitch. Sorry I can't be more helpful. By the way, do you have to wear those pants? They're so dorky."

The Uncool Approach

So how does an Uncool Mom deal with those heartrending moments when her daughter is in tears because of some other kids' venom? As I mentioned earlier, you have to mentally step away. Don't go near that tinderbox of your old teen emotions, or risk being consumed by repressed anger. Remember that what your daughter needs right now is not a partner in hysteria or a co-victim; neither will help her handle the stress or gain a rational perspective on this time of her life. Be a comfort to her, calmly acknowledging these three truths: the unfairness of the situation, the unquestionable fault of the offending (and unprovoked) classmate, and that said classmate is a slime mold.

"Hold on there," you say. "By advocating that another child be demoted five or six phyla, wouldn't I, in fact, be a partner in hysteria?" Not at all. Invariably your wounded child will want to verbally lash out at her attacker in the safety of her own home, and if she thinks the girl's a slime mold, who are you to disagree?

So let her rage. Much like the tantrums she had when she was tiny, these tirades help her get the anger out of her system. She'll probably spew forth some pretty vicious and abusive bile that you never believed could pass through those angel lips that until recently covered your face in soft little kisses. It's shocking whenever it happens, and you might next be expecting your little pumpkin's head to do a Linda Blair spin, but before you jump to any conclusion that involves the devil or the irrevocable end to your sweetie-pie's sweetness, consider the psychologically and hormonally confused state of the young teen.

The stress of trying to figure out who she is and where she fits in, as well as riding the wild mood swings due to never-before-felt hormonal changes, are enough to make anyone lose it. Not only does the teen have to manage all that, but she also has to do well in school, deal with zits, wonder if she'll ever get married, and cope with annoying parents. When you add the social equivalent of a sledgehammer attack in the mix, it's a wonder she doesn't sprout scaly ridges down her back and lay waste to Tokyo. Considering everything, a little rancor and a few virulent outbursts seem positively restrained.

But *My* Daughter's a Nice Girl

Your daughter may be sweet at home or to her friends, but I swear that behind every middle school girl (including my own—and yours) there lurks the potential to send a less popular wretch home in tears. I would bet that every girl between the ages of eleven and seventeen has at some time snubbed or given a dirty look to a socially more vulnerable classmate without provocation.

Our Clueless Mom might answer, "I'm sorry, you have the wrong child—my daughter, Spiffy, reads to blind orphaned senior citizens." Someone in a nursing home is not the same as an unpopular girl who would threaten Spiffy's social status if Spiffy so much as talked to her. The result? At best a silent snub; at worst actively making fun of the poor girl behind her back or to her face.

And Best Bud? She too might falsely see her daughter as immune to the cruelty that is endemic to her age group, or she might justify her daughter's behavior by claiming that her princess was the injured party when in fact she might have been the aggressor. The ultimate Best Bud reaction, if her child is an indisputable social queen, is to shrug it off because nasty behavior is the nature of life in middle school—there's nothing anyone can do about it. (Of course condemning such conduct and trying to raise her child's consciousness is just out of the question.)

But My Husband and I Were Both Unpopular

What should you do if you somehow gave birth to a popular girl? It's not impossible, even if in high school you were voted Most Likely to Die Friendless. I'm convinced that popularity is a recessive gene, like blue eyes or blonde hair, and even more coveted since there are no social equivalents to hair dye and colored contact lenses that can "fix" what your DNA failed to give you. Somewhere on your family tree someone was popular—maybe Great-great-great Grandma Brandi, who was Queen Bee of her one-room schoolhouse, insouciantly flipping the strings of her bonnet and slurring, "whate'er!" when told to churn more butter.

Regardless of our children's social status, we all have a responsibility to train them to be kind—even to social rejects. If our child is popular, it is actually a more pressing obligation. Female bullying has become such an epidemic among our youth (the Sesame Street generation—obviously all those Big Bird songs about the importance of being nice really paid off) that we, the parents, must help the schools eradicate it.

Solutions

What if your daughter is on the receiving end of brutality? When her emotional wound isn't so fresh and she's willing to talk about a solution to an ongoing crisis with an archenemy or a more recent problem with a brand new social blister, then the two of you can put your heads together to come up with some answers. They may include a change in your daughter's approach to her adversary, a trip to the guidance counselor, and/or recognition that adolescence is probably the worst time in a girl's life, but it doesn't last very long.

When my brothers and I were kids and one of us would be upset about something that we really couldn't do anything about, our mother would help the victim du jour spin out all the vengeful things we'd do to our antagonist if we made the rules and ran the world. Now when I said she "helped," I don't mean that she rolled up her sleeves and started plotting the downfall of some fourth-grader herself; she only provided the listening board and helped us in maneuvering our anger so we could get it out of our systems.

So I use this technique with my daughter as long as it seems to be settling her and not adding more bitter refuse on the dumpsite of grudges. If this sounds like I'm getting on her level à la Best Bud Mom and diving into the toxic waters of middle school vengeance, fear not. The point isn't to feed her bile; it's to let the bile that's already there out. If she devises an imaginary counterstrike that's especially original, I'm there to admire her ingenuity; if she comes up with a comeuppance that's hilarious, I'm there to laugh; and if she concocts a reprisal that's a little too bloodthirsty, I'm there to curb her enthusiasm and jostle awake her moral conscience. But most important, I'm there.

Writing Wrongs

If your daughter is not the type to talk about the traumatic social events at school, or if, for whatever reason, she doesn't respond to my mother's method, there are other helpful exercises you can encourage her to try.

Because my daughter loves to write, it was easy to recommend that she write down her loathsome middle school encounters to be used in some hard-hitting short story later on. After she's had a chance to complain or be upset, I'll say, "Use this experience to your advantage: Write down what happened and all the pain you're going through so that you'll always be able to remember exactly how you feel at this moment. These girls may think that they're hurting you, but they actually just gave you material."

Of course, not every girl loves to write as much as my

daughter does, but I'd bet that many would feel better if they just jotted down their feelings in a poem, a journal, or a diary (or illustrate them in a drawing), which they can show you or not, depending on their sense of privacy. Let them know that the point isn't that it has to be good; the point is for them to express themselves, which will help take the edge off the emotional pain and slough off that oppressive feeling of powerlessness. Even when my daughter doubts that she would ever want to use her miserable experiences in her writing, I suggest that it might be useful to refer to it some day in the future when her daughter goes through her own social misery with Xenor455, the most popular android in school.

Manna from Heaven

Sometimes the most outrageous retribution against a malevolent classmate comes not out of your daughter, but out of the blue. On occasion, the gods of Cosmic Justice can settle the score with such an exquisitely ruthless method that the two of you can just sit back and enjoy the consequent hullabaloo.

That was our experience a couple of years ago. One of the popular girls threw a huge party, inviting everyone in the grade except for a few unlucky souls, including my daughter. She was crushed; I was annoyed and stupefied: Didn't the mother realize how hurt and devastated the several kids who were left out would feel? The party came and went, but a few days later it was revealed, much to the excluded girls' delight, that their Guardian Angels teamed up and left all the attendees with a most unwelcome party favor: lice. What a sublime and satisfying outcome. My daughter and I spent a few weeks marveling over God's wisdom, fair-mindedness, and puckish sense of humor.

Why We Have Ears

For those of us whose parenting beliefs include nonstop yammering to a young child in order to develop her verbal mechanics and vocabulary, shutting up and listening is a skill we've never even tried to master. By adolescence a child's ability to express herself is developed enough, as demonstrated by any time a phone attaches itself to her head, suggesting that now is a good time to stop the verbal barrage. Maybe it's time we try listening—ears open, mouth shut—and not shooting back an automatic answer to try to make things all better. As my daughter once blurted at me when I was trying to smooth over a bad day she had, "Can't you just be quiet and listen to me for a change?"

I think there's a tendency for us to chatter away at our kids, trying to convince them that things aren't so bad. We want to make the situation better right away so that our beloved angels don't feel pain, but social injuries are not booboos you can kiss away. Nor are they annoying dust balls that can be swept away by changing the topic to something cheerier, or by taking her on a trip to the sweet shop. Once a girl is past the age of ten, no amount of ice cream can soothe her damaged ego, that is, until she's about twenty and she figures out that a quart of Haagen Dazs chocolate-chocolate chip is peerless as an emotional Valium.

Heartache is an unavoidable fact of life, and shielding your adolescent from the pain in her life is depriving her of the opportunity to learn how to handle her own problems, as well as make decisions on how to solve them, both of which are important elements of growing up. When a child goes through a difficult period and receives the careful guidance of a comforting adult, she will develop empathy enough to refrain from inflicting misery on others. This will get her nowhere in the upper echelons of American business, but it will make her a better person.

Lean on Me

The main point here is that by listening and comforting your daughter in a completely nonjudgmental manner, you are establishing yourself as someone she can really talk to when in need without fear of interruption, rejection, criticism, or condescension. Don't think that such a connection between the two of you will hinder her separating from you; she'll just know whom she can trust and rely on during the social hells of school, until she is ready to stand on her own and move on.

Besides, everyone, regardless of age, could use a little unconditional love.

Dr. Ava says:

As this chapter emphasizes, your role as the Uncool Mom of an adolescent is going to be sorely tested when you see your daughter headed for trouble at school. But remember, failure is a powerful teacher, and she would be better off failing early in life (preferably even before she hits high school) when the consequences to her are much less significant. After all, no one will ever ask your daughter how well she did in sixth grade (Maybe the FBI?), but flunking out of college is going to be hard to explain—and even harder if the answer is, "My mom used to help me with my homework."

Of course, what mom can stand by and watch her teenager slip beneath the waves? The trick here is to stand on shore, throw her a lifeline, and get her to swim. (If you jump in the water with her, you're both lost.) How can you help your sinking scholar?

Be realistic about your daughter's academic potential. There are many different kinds of intelligence—physical, mathematical, verbal, spatial, mechanical, emotional, creative, and so on—and not all of them show up in conventional school settings. (How many professional athletes, choreographers, artists, chefs, and film directors were A students?) The background of many truly creative people is littered with school failures in math, foreign languages, and history, for example—but they went on to achieve at high levels in their chosen careers once they were given the chance.

Encourage and emphasize your daughter's strengths. Not every child is going to be (nor should she be) "well-rounded." A poor math student may excel at art; a great tennis player may have trouble with history. Make sure that you and your daughter know where her strengths lie and help her to pursue them while shoring up her weaknesses. Were you great at everything in school? (I got the highest marks on verbal tests and was abysmal at math. It didn't stop me from accomplishing anything in life except balancing my checkbook.)

Make sure your daughter's academic struggles don't reflect hidden learning disabilities. We all have abilities and disabilities (anyone who wears glasses or contact lenses, for example, is visually disabled), but we know much more now about how learning problems compromise the school performance of lots of kids. A teen who's described as "lazy," "disorganized," "dreamy," or "flaky," for example, might really have underlying learning problems with concentration, executive functioning of the brain, attention deficits, or sequential thinking. Don't assume you know the reasons for your daughter's school problems; they may require professional help.

Finally, remember that for every teen who's lucky enough to be living out *Happy Days,* there's one for whom *Welcome to the Dollhouse* is a more truthful depiction of her daily life. And there's not much you can do about it. Whether your daughter is a Queen Bee, Wannabe, or Don't Wannabe, she must still confront the social complexities and manipulations of adolescence—the alliances, the best friends, the betrayals, the gossip, the bullying, the rejections, the reprieves, all of it, alone.

Nothing can make a teenager more miserable than an awful (or absent) social life, and this is where your perspective can really make a difference. (Just the fact that you survived adolescence counts for a lot.) But as this chapter points out, you can't be so identified with your daughter's distress that you become a helpless co-victim along with her, nor can you become equally overwhelmed and share in her hysteria and agitation.

Instead, this is a good opportunity to make use of what I call the four Cs —Compassion, Communication, Comprehension, and Competence. Using these key words to initiate and keep the conversation going between you and your daughter will provide her with the kind of support she can use right now. Here's how it works:

1. **Compassion**—Always open the conversation with empathy. For example, "Wow, it sounds as if Louise said some really harsh things to you," instead of "What'd you say to get Louise so angry?"

2. **Communication**—Follow your compassionate opening with a neutral inquiry into the circumstances of the event. For instance, "Tell me everything you remember about the fight, so I really understand what happened." Don't dismiss or deny your daughter's feelings ("Forget about it. In a week you won't even remember this fight.").

3. **Comprehension**—Once you've heard what happened, restate the event in your own words, incorporating your own understanding. "So, as I get it, Louise was angry about your friendship with Marissa, and she felt jealous." Don't try to console your daughter ("Louise is a bitch. You have plenty of other friends.").

4. **Competence**—If you've followed steps 1, 2, and 3, now you have a chance to help your daughter problem-solve and come away from the experience feeling strengthened. For example, "You have a tricky problem here—how to make friends with Marissa while not losing your friendship with Louise. Maybe we can think of some strategies," instead of, "I'm going to call Louise's mother. She should know how badly her daughter's behaving."

13. Beauty and Body

Face it, Mom—no one in our family has ever
been a supermodel.
—Julia, 13

The Pinnacle of Teen Obsession

Teens fret about their bodies and their beauty more than they
fret about anything else in their lives, except maybe popularity.
They seem to be so preoccupied with their looks that they will
spend countless hours on it: One day when driving my daughter to school, I noticed that about 90 percent of the tardy students were perfectly groomed girls. Couldn't they have just
forgone the impossibly smooth ponytail and expert lip-gloss
application and gotten to school on time instead?

Adolescents are at a time in their lives when their bodies
are changing. For some it's exciting; for others, freaky. How
they look, it seems to them, determines everything that makes
teen life worthwhile: what clique they get into, how popular
they are, and if they will ever get a boyfriend. That's a lot of

pressure to put on people so young that, a few years before, they seriously considered "princess" a legitimate career choice for when they grew up.

Right now we live in a beauty-obsessed culture. There are more makeup stores in malls than there are "You are here" maps. And let's not even get started on nail salons. In my area alone, you could go to a different salon for each of your fingernails, and still have a few left over for your toes.

Image Is Everything

For our daughters, life as an impressionable looks-obsessed teen is fraught with not only the typical beauty pressure from their peers, but also far too many demands from society—possibly more than any previous generation has experienced. As Kim S. sees it, "Girls today are expected to work, have a family, and all these things that we do, but now they have to be perfectly gorgeous while they're doing it. I think that they're in a lot of psychological pain now because they don't feel they measure up to the beauty standards of popular culture. And beautiful girls think that their good looks are their only worth."

All this obsessing usually leads to girls developing certain perceptions, or misperceptions as the case may be, about themselves. In their minds, they're too fat, too skinny, too flatchested, too hairy. Their eyes are too small, noses too big, hair too dark, too curly, too straight. For every feature on every girl, there's a flaw to be focused on.

"She's eighty-five pounds," says Karen D. of her thirteen-year-old Haley, "and the other day she told me her thighs were too big." And then there's Barb M.'s daughter Alice, who has a beautiful figure but complains that her thighs are too thin.

And then there's my daughter. She rarely says, "I wish I

had never been born," but she often tells me, "I wish I had never been born with dark hair and dark eyes." She's been known to cavil about her arms, her eyelashes, her ankles, her lips, even her feet, all of which are fine, if not pretty. That's when I say, "Honey, you can't argue with your DNA." She says, "Well, thanks for giving me all the worst genes."

The Student Body

"I'm too fat!" Mothers hear it all the time. It sends waves of uneasiness through our bodies since anorexia has become such an epidemic among teen girls. And yes, some girls do fall prey to that disease, and yes, we should all be as vigilant about anorexia as we are about drug abuse, but I find that a lot of these girls—the healthy ones—say it because it's just the thing to say. Or it's the phantom body concern of the day.

In sixth grade when my sylphlike daughter started up with the fat complaints, I decided to talk to her about the reality of her size (thin), the distorted impressions teens can get about themselves, and the seriousness of anorexia. She admitted that she knew she wasn't fat; she was just saying it to fit in with the rest of the girls. "If I don't say it," she explained, "the other girls will think I'm stuck-up about being thin."

While there may be many girls who feign fat anxieties to conform to their peer group, there are far more who honestly see themselves as overweight even though they aren't.

Sound familiar? Neither svelte nor stocky, this type of teen falls somewhere in the middle body-wise. Although you may see her for what she is—a healthy, average-sized girl—she bemoans the fact that she isn't as thin as, say, a more popular girl at her school or Christina Aguilera. Other than pointing out that Christina Aguilera must be storing some of her internal organs at an off-site warehouse since there's no way she has enough square footage in her body to fit a complete digestive tract, what can you as her Uncool Mom do?

Talking Helps

If your daughter seems obsessed about dieting and is developing bizarre eating habits, get her to a doctor pronto. But if she's just going through garden-variety teen misery about her body image, the best thing to do is to talk with her about it. Teens have a nasty habit of looking at the world in a skewed manner and only sharing it with their equally deluded friends, thereby creating a monster of misinformation that they will believe in whole-heartedly. Just as Dorothy melted the Wicked Witch of the West by drenching her, mothers must periodically pour a bucket of water on some of their daughters' more outlandishly inaccurate theories before they spin out of control.

So get her to talk. Discuss, as I did with my daughter, eating disorders and her health. And here comes the hard part: Do not be judgmental when she insists that she's fat, and *please*, resist the urge to tell her she's being silly, crazy, or impossible. What she needs to hear is reality and acceptance. You may find yourself blue-faced, chanting "You're fine the way you are" in the face of her protestations, but I believe that somewhere in her muddled brain, it's getting through.

If you feel you need more guidance, do not hesitate to contact a psychologist who can supply you with some strategies to help your daughter through this period of body image problems. Also of note are two books on the topic recommended by the *New York Times* health expert Jane Brody: *Bodylove*, by Dr. Rita Freeman; and *Big Fat Lies*, by Dr. Glenn Gaesser.

Oh, and don't be surprised if the day after you have a conversation with your daughter that *you* may have considered fruitful enough to put the issue to rest, she comes back to you complaining that she's fat, as if the previous twenty-four hours were all a figment of your imagination. Words of encouragement and acceptance are like food to a teen: They digest them, metabolize them, and soon need more. So getting angry at having to fill her up again and again with reassurances makes about as much sense as blowing a gasket because she needs dinner every night.

Pound Foolish

So where have our children picked up the message that femininity equals worrying about your weight? The media? Absolutely. When scrawny, bone-thin actresses and models are being heralded as the Helens of Troy of our age, we can rightly point our collective finger at the media. But what about *our* culpability?

We've probably all done it (I know I have): asked our husbands, "Do I look fat in these pants?" or said, "I'm so fat—I've got to lose some weight." We are so used to uttering these thoughts that we don't even realize we've said them, but I'll bet our kids do. Children learn by imitating their elders. Think before you gripe.

A fashionable woman who loves clothes and looking stylish, Joan D. frequently monitors the size of her rump—in front of her daughter Chloe. "My husband says to me, 'Why don't you go check your ass in the mirror in front of your adolescent daughter and mention how fat you think your butt looks one more time? How healthy is that?'"

Now is not the time to jump ship and embrace the Best Bud way of life. Don't teach your kid that constant fad dieting and weight wailing is a ritual that must be observed if one is to become a woman. Not only is it an Uncool no-no, but these actions also emphasize looks too much and can lead to very unhealthful eating habits that could stay with your daughter for the rest of her life. So stop dragging your child down into your petty little calorie-counting hell. There are better ways to approach weight control.

Moderation

I know I mention "moderation" a few times throughout this book, but in the case of attitudes toward eating and weight loss, it's essential. Extremism applied to nutrition can result in some dangerous practices. Even a child who is actually overweight should be given a diet that is moderate in its caloric restrictions—developed and recommended by a doctor or licensed nutritionist.

The Uncool Mom may not be able to control what all the other kids are doing, nor can she censor the media, but what she can do, besides halting her own mirror-reflected butt surveillance, is teach by example the right way to eat. We need to send them the message that they should be comfortable in their own skin, that they shouldn't be so hypercritical of themselves, but also that it's important to stay relatively trim and fit for the sake of their health.

There's another form of moderation that we can all exercise, and that is providing a moderating force to combat the extreme view of the world that the media does present to our children. Stay on top of what magazines your teen is reading and what she's watching on TV. Whenever you catch her admiring the tiny circumference of Celine Dion's triceps or the fact that you could stow a New York City Yellow Pages comfortably in the space between Gwyneth Paltrow's thighs, take that opportunity to discuss with her the cultural myth that one can never be too rich or too thin.

Subtly point out some of the successful women in our society who are not bone-thin yet are still considered beautiful: Oprah, Kate Winslet, food diva Nigella Lawson, Renee Zellweger (as Bridget Jones, not as herself), even Catherine Zeta-Jones, who while slender, still looks like she's had a full meal. And if your daughter responds to this list as my daughter would ("But they're all old, like you"), do what I do: Hit her with a list of teen idols who fill the bill: J-Lo, Drew Barrymore, several of the members in the girl groups Dream and 3LW, actress Hillary Duff (who plays Disney Channel's Lizzy McGuire). These are all successful young women who are secure enough in their talents and beauty to look real.

More to Love?

And what if your teen is in fact overweight? As an Uncool Mom, you should look long and hard at your own behavior before deciding on a course of action regarding your daughter. Ask yourself, "Am I doing anything that may be enabling her to stay heavy?" There are so many ways that a loving mother can subconsciously sabotage weight-loss efforts, from keeping mountains of high-calorie junk food around the house to observing "fun" or "cozy" rituals such as a family movie night replete with candy and buttered popcorn. If you yourself are overweight, do you subconsciously want a partner in obesity in order to normalize your own bad eating habits? Remember that the phrase "the more the merrier" was never meant to include adipose tissue.

So, let's say that you're doing everything right but your

daughter is still too heavy. Your first phone call should be to her pediatrician. A doctor is the most qualified person to tell you just how bad the problem is. You may have thinness standards that are unrealistic for your daughter's body type to attain, or maybe the few extra pounds will most likely be shed once she hits her growth spurt. And if a weight loss and exercise plan is warranted, a doctor will be the best person to determine the right program and the best person to present it to your daughter, since teens rarely rebel against their doctors' orders the way they do against their mothers'.

And most important, remember the value of acceptance. Be careful not to criticize your child when discussing her weight issue. Never make her feel guilty or ugly, and DO NOT nag. These are all behaviors that will send her seeking comfort in the arms of the Keebler elves.

> If your daughter shows any signs of extreme eating behaviors, including uncontrollable bingeing, not eating, or following diets that are very restrictive, consult your doctor as she may have an eating disorder.

Wishing and Waiting

Some teen girls can get very impatient waiting for their bodies to bloom. Breasts, especially large ones, seem to be on the top of every female adolescent's Christmas list. And they're not alone, as the sales in Wonderbras and "figure-enhancing" (i.e., padded) bras, and the rampant practice of surgical breast enlargements, all can attest to. A prowlike chest that is capable of poking people in the eyes when you shake their hands seems to have become a cultural pot o' gold these days.

One thirteen-year-old girl I know, Sarah, is developing physically at a normal rate but still thinks she looks like a little girl. "My breasts could be mistaken for pimples or ingrown hairs," she said. It's understandable. I remember having a young teen fantasy about how someday Sophia Loren and I could time-share bras. The vision that I had was always from my own perspective, and it was always the same: me, in a bikini, walking down the beach to meet my friends, my chin practically resting on two fleshy mounds so big that they obscured the view to my feet. It never happened.

Never-Never Land

Of course, wanting to look like a woman is far preferable to dreading it since it's one of those unavoidable things that happens to girls. Considering that for some adolescents the journey to physical maturity is neither smooth nor eagerly anticipated, the typical infantilizing input of the Clueless Mom is, quite frankly, overkill. Mrs. Clueless, with her penchant for not acknowledging that her little Polly Pocket playmate will soon turn into a potential Playboy Playmate, can often cast growing up in either a negative or mysterious light. Some of these moms might brush aside, or worse, laugh at, a young girl's desire to wear a training bra. Instead of letting her daughter dip her toes into puberty just to get a feel for it, Clueless makes the whole thing verboten, as if to say, "You? Growing up? Only when I give you permission."

Obviously, this approach is psychologically damaging, especially when it extends to silence about menstrual periods. I heard from one mother whose daughter reported that several of her friends never had conversations with their moms about getting their periods. What a confusing and frightening experience for a girl to get her period when she hasn't been prepared for it. Sure, the schools tell them everything they need to know, but nothing replaces a one-on-one with Mom. Just because the schools give kids lunch, does that mean we don't have to feed them at home?

I Enjoy Being a Girl

Because I did not embrace getting my period with the same zeal that I had for growing milk glands large enough to feed an orphanage, I was determined to be as enthusiastic as possible about it with my daughter. I discussed it with her since she was very young, and she's been looking forward to getting her period since she was about seven. Fortunately for all those involved, it happened many years later. She was so excited when it came that she screamed in the bathroom as if she had just won a beauty pageant. She ran to me, tears of excitement bubbling at the corners of her eyes, and burst out, "I can't believe it—I can have babies!" "Not on my watch," I shot back.

Shocking proclamations aside, I'm thrilled that she sees becoming a woman as a wonderful thing. The only concern I had was how on earth she was going to take care of herself and her environs. She shares a bathroom with her little brother (then six), and I was afraid that every time "her friend came," the place would look like a crime scene. My fears were unfounded; she's very clean and careful. Interestingly enough, getting her period matured her in a way that my nagging never could.

The Zit Offensive

If you had a bad complexion as an adolescent, you probably are very conscious of how your daughter's skin is shaping up.

Afraid that the chromosomal apple doesn't fall far from the family tree, the acne veteran is more likely going to be on the case before there is even much of a case. But that doesn't mean that your daughter will listen. You can lead a teen to water, but you can't make her wash.

"I had crummy skin as a kid, and I wanted to prevent Jackie from that heartache," says Renée C., "so I buy her all this stuff and show her how to use it. I try to give her guidance hoping that I might eliminate the pain she could endure from her peers, but she doesn't care." Renée has since gone the Uncool route and decided that she'll keep buying the products and tossing them into the bathroom, but it's up to Jackie to use them.

Other Skin Problems

Let's say your daughter's skin has been treated effectively. She goes out with her friends one night, her crystal-clear complexion shining like the sun, but the next morning you catch a glimpse of something colorful under her pajamas—a tattoo. Or maybe when she puts on a top from her endless supply of navel-baring shirts, you notice a new addition to her tummy— a belly button ring. What's an Uncool Mom to do?

First of all, realize that, like it or not, times change. We may just have to face up to the fact that our culture is now embracing body adornments that in our generation were considered sleazy. Margo R., whose daughter came home from college with a tattoo, tried to comfort her husband with these words: "You and I are members of the last generation to have undecorated skin. People will point at it some day and wonder why we are so strange."

Mom's Rules for Sleazy Body Jewelry

So while Clueless Mom would just forbid all skin decoration (possibly resulting in the teen or her friend trying to do it themselves—an engraved invitation for bacteria to visit indefinitely) and Best Bud would give her daughter carte blanche to pierce every square inch of her body (and may also tag along to get matching mother/daughter nipple rings), the Uncool Mom has to find that middle ground: allowing some things, but not without a little supervision. She knows that like most other privileges in a teen's life, there's a time and a place and a rule for everything. Just as I have Mom's rules for Appropriate Attire, I've got some for this area too.

1. *Additional earlobe holes*: There are no medical reasons to forbid it and it's part of the culture now. If she wants to look like a pirate, so what? As long as she pays for it, keeps it clean, and buys the matching sets of earrings, it's okay with me. But she had better clear it with me first, or she'll have to let it grow back.

2. *Ear cartilage*: Thank God I live in New York State, which has a law requiring anyone under the age of sixteen to have a parent present during any kind of cartilage piercing, but that means I only have two and a half years left of this kind of state-sanctioned peace of mind. When she turns sixteen, my daughter will have to earn her cartilage piercings by showing me responsibility. I could happily trade a couple of rings at the top of her ear for a year of honor-roll grades.

3. *Belly button piercing*: Personally, I completely understand the appeal of belly button rings and bars. There's a lot of fun jewelry out there just for navels, and my daughter knows it. Again, it's a privilege she must earn. Sixteen seems like a good age to impale one's navel with a needle, and as long as

she asks permission, pays for it, gets it done at a reputable place, and keeps it clean, it's okay with me. Unlike many other types of body piercings, it's not something that would show in a job interview (unless she's interviewing to be a lifeguard or stripper, and somehow I don't think it would hurt her chances with either).

4. *Other piercings (eyebrows, nose, tongue) and tattoos*: I'm trying to discourage these things by talking to my daughter now about how people make snap judgments about others based on the way they dress, the way they speak, the way they carry themselves, and where they choose to poke holes in their bodies. Luckily she's interested enough in her future to understand (at thirteen anyway—talk to me in a couple of years) that maybe it will be easier to have college interviews without a glob of metal stuck in her tongue. If she changes her mind, these are things that she will only be allowed to get once she's eighteen. Actually, when she's eighteen, she'll be able to get tattoos one weekend and then pierce them the next if she wants—she'll be too old to stop.

5. *General Rules:* Once my daughter starts showing interest in looking like a pincushion, I'm going to make known a few general rules. Piercing permission is granted with the understanding that I can determine that certain earrings, studs, and so on come out for certain events. And if she ever tries to bypass rules 1 through 4, whatever hole she got has to grow back and she will never be given permission for another.

The one thing I'm going to try to keep in mind about all these skin decorations is this: It's not my skin; it's not my life. And if your daughter has already inserted multiple rings in her body, remember that for every cloud there's a silver lining, and the silver lining here is that you can always creep into her room while she's sleeping, tie strings on every one of those little rings, and then lead her around like a cow. Well, maybe not, but it makes a good threat.

Removable Skin Decoration

Makeup—the Crayola crayons of grown women everywhere. All the colors, all the possibilities—its charms are endless, and teens quickly fall under its spell. Our task is to try to help them learn how to wear makeup so that they're not mistaken for hookers. Some kids solve that problem by smuggling the makeup into school and putting it on there so that they just look like hookers going to algebra.

When Valerie B. was growing up, her mother was very strict about teens wearing makeup, so Valerie used to sneak it on when she was riding the bus to school. As a result, she was determined to bring her daughter Caroline, thirteen, up in an atmosphere that was cosmetics-friendly. An admitted makeup freak who's on a first-name basis with the Chanel counter girl, she does have a few rules: "I think anyone her age wearing Chanel is just idiotic. No dark colors, mascara, or eyeliner yet, but she does have age-appropriate lip gloss, blush, and sparkling things that are okay."

Valerie has a smart technique for keeping her daughter from dallying with the prohibited colors and tools: During sleepovers, when all the girls go into a makeover frenzy, she allows them to rummage through her old cosmetics drawer. Valerie hit on a great Uncool Mom solution: moderation. Makeup has not become an issue because she never made it an issue.

Time Necessary to Apply Makeup
(in a one-day period)

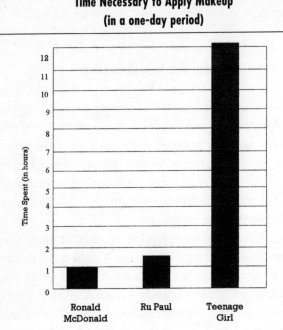

Girls with a Purpose

No matter what attitude you have and no matter how moderate your approach, some girls still refer to *The Rocky Horror Picture Show* as a makeup primer. Leila Y. has a daughter whose personality dictated that she just had to be extreme in her looks. "Camilla went to a small private school, K-12. When she was sixteen, she wore so much eye makeup, including heavy, heavy mascara, that the principal called and asked her to tone it down—she was scaring the first graders." She toned it down. (This is an excellent example of letting the school play the heavy.)

And then there's Michelle V. whose daughter decided to

do something a little different with her hair while her mom was out one day. Michelle came home and caught Heather in the bathroom. Behind a closed door, she admitted that she had dyed her hair, and when Michelle asked, "What color?" Heather threw the box out: Fuchsia—and permanent. At first upset, Michelle then realized, "What can you do? The deed was done. She came out, and all I could say was, 'Interesting color.' Since then she's dyed her hair about a million times. And I realized there was nothing to be done because it's just hair."

Less Desirable Hair

If you think that the color and style of her tresses are the only subject of hair arguments you can have with your daughter, you are sorely mistaken. As much as she is obsessed with making the most of the hairs on her head, she is equally preoccupied with getting rid of those that dare to grow on her body.

Tweezing, plucking, shaving, waxing, bleaching—these are all aspects of an issue that plagues many young girls and their mothers. And my sense is that it's an issue that's more than follicle deep.

A lot of us don't want our kids growing up too quickly, and maybe to us, hair removal is a practice that seems a little too grown-up. Quite frankly, it's a little discomfiting to be buying razors and waxing kits for someone who only recently you supplied with Colgate's Looney Tunes toothpaste.

Maybe the problem with the image of our daughter's shaving, waxing, and so forth, has something to do with why women remove unwanted hair—to look attractive and sexy to men. So perhaps it's the association with sexuality that subconsciously creeps out so many moms about their daughters' depilatory obsessions.

And so the conflict continues: What moms see as the silky down of a late summer peach, daughters see as Castro's beard. But be careful of drawing a line in the sand. It's easy for a girl to disobey any hair-removal injunctions by taking the matter into her own hands, oftentimes with dubious results.

Take the story of Sally. Determined to look her best for her family's vacation in Florida, she defied her mother and furtively tried perfecting her eyebrows. In her opinion, all they needed was a little thinning, and the best way to achieve that, she thought, was by applying Nair. Once the deed was done, she came crying from the bathroom with a towel over her head, straight into her mother's arms. Reluctantly pulling back the towel, she revealed a completely eyebrowless face—absolutely nothing framing her red, tear-gushing eyes.

You Can't Spell *Space Cadet* without *Spa*

Leave it to the Best Bud Moms to provide us with the worst method of dealing with this time in our daughters' lives—professional spa procedures. Maybe I'm alone on this one, but regularly taking a teenager to a chic day spa for a fifty- or sixty-dollar waxing, shaping, and tweezing festival is, well, really bone-headed. It's a little disturbing for kids to think that the only way to deal with an unwanted hair is to pay someone else to remove it.

The one legitimate exception would be for the girl whose eyebrows are so thick and unruly that they pose a daunting challenge to the amateur plucker. A professional may be needed to show the girl and her mother just how to shape and tame them, but a single visit should do the job. It's important that the daughter knows that it's a one-time treat. Presenting the salon trip as a special rite of passage is one way to enjoy the experience without letting her think that regular costly visits are a new after-school activity.

A Happy Medium

An approach more moderate than the preceding is to allow your growing girl to shave, pluck, and so on, but at first under your gentle supervision. As she gets older, an adolescent should feel that she has more and more control over aspects of her life, and beauty procedures provide the Uncool Mom with a great opportunity to give her that control gradually (emphasis on *gradually*).

If she feels that you're supportive of her desire to look her best (as defined by her somewhat skewed teen sensibilities), she'll know that you don't want to keep her from growing up; on the contrary, she'll know that you respect the new person she's becoming. Let her know that you think she's fine just the way she is, but if plucking or shaving or waxing will make her more comfortable, you'll be there to help. Of course, you don't actually need to tell her that you'll also be there to prevent her from going overboard and ending up looking like an alien. With this approach, who knows? You might even be able to talk her out of her more bizarre notions of personal beauty, such as dyeing her hair fuchsia.

Finally, it's important to remember that just because you don't see the need for hair removal doesn't mean that it's not real to your daughter. Take Lisa S. After months of arguments, she finally let her daughter Tori, thirteen, do something about her "mustache" (as the girl called it). "I couldn't see it, but it really bothered Tori." So Lisa has helped her wax the phantom mustache for a year now. Tori feels confident and really appreciates her mom taking her seriously. Even so, says Lisa, "It's hard to keep a straight face when a girl who still gets chocolate all over her mouth can be so concerned about what her upper lip looks like."

Teenagers Are Only Skin Deep

Thinking over why I had reservations about my daughter plucking her eyebrows, I came to the realization that the core of my resistance was centered on the following questions: If I allow her to change her appearance, then what message am I sending about her beauty—that it's not good enough? That she needs to look perfect and like everyone else to be valuable? Am I saying to her that she is in fact defective and unattractive in her natural state? And most important, am I perpetuating one of the American culture's most destructive myths—that a woman's self-worth and societal worth should be tied up with her beauty?

Well, surprise! In junior high (and for some, senior high) society, self-worth is very much tied up with how you look. Beauty is very important to young teens. It probably always has been, and it probably always will be, unless in the future we're all robots. You can't change the adolescent fixation on appearance any more than you can change the fact that no matter what nymphlike image is reflected when they look in a mirror, they will notice only their defects. Don't you remember how dissatisfied you were with even your tiniest flaws at that time in your life? Don't you wish you now looked a little more the way you did then?

Remembrances of Things Past

It's an unfortunate convergence that as we age, we have daughters who are beautiful in the way only teenagers can be, but who constantly trash their looks. As my daughter reaches the stage in her life marked by microscopic scrutiny and analysis of every imperfection (real or imagined) found on her face and body, I am reaching the age where, in terms of looks, it's all downhill from here. I realize that from now on, the only way I'm ever going to turn heads in public is if I collapse onto the pavement needing immediate medical attention. Accordingly, I'm starting to adopt a more Zen-like approach to physical beauty or lack thereof (making a virtue of necessity). I'm saying—or trying to believe anyway—that looks don't matter anymore; it's what's inside that counts.

Just as you're convincing yourself that this is true, you notice your perfectly beautiful daughter criticizing her own appearance when all you can see is the youthful, dewy suppleness of her complexion, the tight skin and muscle of her triceps, a perky and firm bustline that doesn't need an underwire bra to keep it in the same zip code as her rib cage. It's hard to be Zen with a teenage girl around the house.

Unfair Comparisons

You listen to your daughter go on about how hideous she is, and then you catch a glimpse of your aging self in the mirror and—"Whoa! Who's that gargoyle?" Or worse, "Mom! What are you doing here?" Or even worse, "Isn't Irene Ryan dead?" If your teen sees herself as so unappealing, you must think, "How must she see me? Is that how everyone sees me? Yikes!"

My daughter, at the ripe age of thirteen, loves to complain

that she has "laugh lines." She has them when she laughs, while I have them constantly. She complains that her arms are too thin, while if my triceps were any more lax, they would qualify as wings. She complains about the color of her hair as my hair loses color. When she complained about the fullness of her cheeks, I realized she was complaining about collagen!

Forever Young

With all this swirling around your graying head, it's easy to respond by trying to deny the encroaching years. Some of us deal with middle age by trying to act younger, be younger, look younger. It's a prime Best Bud trap that results in a woman who should know better acting as if she doesn't. I must admit, only the toughest and most resolved Uncool Moms are immune to the infectious spread of the desire to stay twenty-five.

Maybe we're all hanging on to the Dove dishwashing liquid commercial of the late '60s, in which the teenage girl's young stud boyfriend "Bud" approaches a sexy woman from behind and pinches her ass. The woman turns around and— shockers! It's his girlfriend's mom! "Sorry, Mrs. Anderson, I thought you were Suzy," Bud spits out. (Her hands didn't give her away, as the announcer so kindly informs us.) But Mrs. Anderson is obviously thrilled—Dove, as well as Bud, made her day.

But do we really want to seduce our daughters' boyfriends? I personally would prefer a guy without braces or an only recently abandoned Pokemon collection. The truth is, we've already had our moment; it's their turn to be in the spotlight now. Moms, it's time to get off the stage.

Mature Beauty

Now before you go saying, "Oh, I get it, the Uncool Mom has to look like an unapologetic hag," let me get something straight. Just because we are mothers of teenagers does not mean that we have to give up and look like turnip-selling babushkas for the rest of our lives. Hardly. It's okay to try to look your best, but it's our responsibility to pursue beauty in an age-appropriate way. The problem lies in trying to reclaim a former glory. We all must embrace the fact that middle-aged as well as older women can in fact be beautiful, but it is a mature beauty that should not be compared to the youthful beauty of teens and twenty-somethings.

Believe it or not, your getting older gracefully, accepting the changes that aging brings, not trying to freeze yourself at an earlier decade, and looking good in a more mature, easygoing, and less perfectionist way is actually psychologically healthy for your daughter. If we become so high maintenance that we expend far too much energy trying to stave off a tiny wrinkle or an extra pound, what message are we sending our daughters? We're telling them, "Yes, beauty is the most important thing in the world!" Show your daughter that women are made of more than their looks.

"Help! I've Given Birth to a Bimbo!"

Most of us want our daughters to be independent, self-actualized, high-achieving, high-self-esteemed, *Our Bodies, Our Selves,* free-from-societal-stereotypes, "nothing's-going-to-hold-me-back" kinds of women. But let's face it—right now they're all pretty vapid, and it's because they're so young. We can't expect them to be tough or wise enough to reject the ideals of their secondary school society right now.

So how do we keep our daughters from permanently having the depth of one-coat, quick-dry nail polish? Obviously, there are no guarantees. What seems to work for the Uncool Mom is to establish priorities in the family early on. In our family, trying your hardest at school is a number one priority, and my daughter hears on a regular basis that by doing well, going to a good college, and ultimately getting a good job, when she is an adult she can have her entire body waxed weekly for all I care, but she'll be able to afford it herself. Whatever the family's priorities are, they should help her in defining her self-worth early enough in her life that she internalizes it.

Not Just Another Pretty Face

Ever since she was tiny, my husband and I have encouraged our daughter to appreciate all facets of what makes her special, such as what she's good at and what she enjoys, rather than how pretty she is. (By the way, I believe a father's participation in this is crucial. It is so important for a girl to get male approval early on that is based on aspects about her character other than her appearance.) Now, we certainly didn't skimp on telling her how cute or pretty she was, but we never let her think that prettiness alone was enough. Our heartiest cheers were saved for things she did—her accomplishments, her interests, her kind-heartedness—so that she understood that a person is the sum of her parts, not just her body parts.

At thirteen my daughter is age-appropriately obsessed with her appearance, but I know that deep down she sees herself as much more. Although she struggles with me about hair color, makeup, and other beauty treatments, I can tell she defines herself as a smart student, a talented writer and artist, a friend to the downtrodden at her school, and an original spirit. As long as I know that her accomplishments, interests, and personal character are at the core of her self-image, I feel a little more comfortable in letting her indulge in many more beauty requests. Except a tongue piercing.

Set an Example

Beyond bringing them up to value all aspects of themselves, the best thing we can do to show our daughters that they're worth more than their looks is to show them that we, their mothers, are worth more than our looks (well-preserved, fading, or otherwise). Sure, during this difficult time in their lives, daughters are going to rebel and try to define themselves by being different from their moms, but I still think it's possible to send a message that they'll notice (not that they'll admit it) and maybe even absorb (which they will never admit). The desired result may not manifest itself until your teen is in her twenties, but timing is not the issue here.

It is now common knowledge that kids whose parents don't smoke are considerably less likely to smoke themselves. That statistic is evidence that children, even teens, will choose behavior that their parents promote by example, unless the behavior in question is collecting all of Sting's albums. Conduct yourself in a particular manner from the time they are born, and that message will become part of their fiber. If you think that sounds too hard, try living with a teenager whose pet name for you is Hypocrite.

Let Loose

So, act like you're worth more than your looks. Don't wail when your nail breaks. Don't obsess about your weight. Don't fret over a stray hair. Never say that you can't go out of the house without (1) makeup, (2) blown-out hair, (3) completely stubble-free lower limbs, (4) a manicure, (5) a pedicure. You can. And you should. Ever notice that no one ever says, "Oh! I can't go out of the house without having read *Moby Dick*!"

We're always telling (and being told to tell) our kids to be individuals. To make that stick, we should be brave enough to be individuals ourselves. Go on. It may sound shocking, but do it: Go grocery shopping without a swab of makeup on. Pick up your kid at school with a chipped nail. Go swimming—get your hair wet and let it dry naturally. Play ball, take a walk in the woods, garden and don't care if you get dirt under your nails or smudges on your face. Get involved in something that takes you out of yourself—a creative hobby, charity work, and so on. Look like a million bucks as often as you need to, but every now and then, try looking like yourself. These little acts of abandon will show your daughter, by example, that life is much more than beauty. And if nothing else, you'll at least be a whole lot more fun.

Dr. Ava says:

Many of the truly funny anecdotes in this chapter actually reveal your daughter's anxieties about her body. This isn't surprising given the fact that our society's ideals for female beauty have moved from voluptuous Marilyn Monroe (your daughter will think she's fat!) to skinny Calista Flockhart (your daughter will think she's just right!). But most girls will not weigh in under a hundred pounds, nor would we want them to. How can you help your daughter feel comfortable with who she is and escape the tyranny of always wanting to be something she's not?

You can start by understanding that we all have five basic fears—fear of the unknown, fear of being alone, fear about the body, fear of the voice of conscience, and fear about the self. These five fears lurk under the surface of even the simplest events in your daughter's life—going to school, shopping at the mall, meeting friends at the park, playing soccer, throwing a party, and so on. For example, let's take going to school. Here's how the five fears can easily turn an ordinary day into a teenage nightmare:

1. **Fear of the unknown:** Will Mr. Lesser give us a test in Spanish? Will Samantha be a bitch again like she was yesterday?
2. **Fear of being alone:** Will anyone sit with me at lunch? Will David like that stuck-up Ashley better than me?
3. **Fear about the body:** Are my thighs too fat? Why can't my hair be straight instead of curly? (As this chapter shows, this is a biggie!)
4. **Fear of the voice of conscience:** Will my mom find out that no one's home at Brian's house? What's the big deal if I cut a few classes to hang out with Anna?
5. **Fear about the self:** I want to be smart and do well, but does that mean I'm a nerd? If I'm friends with Nicki, do I have to go as far as she does with boys? If I don't, will she think I'm a wimp?

Is there anything you can do to help your daughter deal with our youth-obsessed, thin-obsessed, beauty-obsessed culture?

Your best bet is to expose her to your own healthier values and provide a real-life model for her behavior. (Alas, this is easier said than done since there doesn't seem to be a woman alive who doesn't wish she were ten pounds lighter.)

Here are three tips that may help:

1. Share negative feelings about your weight, your hair, and your wrinkles with other moms, *not your daughter*. (This is a special warning for Best Bud Moms.)

2. Implement healthy eating and exercising in your home for everyone rather than constant dieting and inactivity.

3. Don't focus on your daughter's beauty or her body as her ticket to success, even (or particularly) if your daughter *is* beautiful. Instead, highlight *all* the attributes your daughter possesses—her brains, her sense of humor, her compassion, her athleticism, and so on. By appreciating your daughter as a whole person, you enable her to *become* a whole person.

14. Boys

I love it that you hate the boy I like!
—*my daughter, 13*

The Rules of the Game

When my daughter was in seventh grade and brought home her first boyfriend, I gave her one rule:

1. Keep the door to your bedroom open at all times.

She gave me six:

1. Do not make jokes about Nickelodeon cartoons or anything else juvenile.
2. Do not speak in the voice that you use when you pretend that the dog talks.
3. Do not dress up or wear anything embarrassing.
4. Do not hang around us. (Stay away.)

5. Do not curse. *[?]*
6. Do not tell dirty jokes. *[?!]*

The first two are legitimate requests. The third just reveals how much more important the event was to her than to me. The fourth shows how much she doesn't want me involved. The last two are real head-scratchers because I rarely curse (only when I'm really, really angry or when a heavy object lands on my foot), and I never tell dirty jokes in front of my kids. Gross ones, yes, to entertain my six-year-old son, but a gross jokes injunction would fall under rule #1 as "anything juvenile." What did she mean by this?

Rules #1 and #2

First of all, she was just nervous. But by analyzing these rules, I think we can infer what she really means: Be invisible. Harry Potter may need a special cloak to be invisible, but I'm an Uncool Mom—I can become invisible at will!

Look at rules #1 and #2—no juvenile references and no buffoonery. Why are these two activities so contraindicated when in the presence of a boyfriend? Because by acting silly and childish, I would be acting the part of the Clueless Mom. I'd be sending the message that I still see her as a "little" girl, at a time when every girl, whether she be skinny, chunky, bespectacled, or orthodontically braced, wants to be in her boyfriend's eyes a *Sports Illustrated* swimsuit model.

As difficult as it may be to accept that image of your daughter (just writing it made me briefly catatonic), it's essential to remember that having a boyfriend is a big step toward a girl having her own life that revolves around her own world. At thirteen, my daughter's life with her family is still a little more important to her than life with her friends. But if everything goes as it should, the relative significance of her family will shrink as that of her peers grows, until finally, when she reaches adulthood, we, her parents, will become satellites orbiting around a world of her own making—a world filled with friends, enemies, lovers, coworkers, her job, her fun, and hopefully a phone call home once a week.

Rule #3

When I first heard rule #3 commanding me not to dress up or wear anything embarrassing, I was amused. I kept imagining this clammy-handed twelve-year-old boy dressed in baggy jeans and T-shirt ringing the kitchen doorbell to be greeted by me in a floor-length Oscar night number, the porch light hitting the crystal beading on my décolleté bodice and refracting into a shimmering explosion of sparkles that dance off our Mr. Coffee. "Bonsoir, " I would lilt, "Please, let me get you a drink—Squirt or Yoo-hoo?"

The real meaning of rules #1, #2, and #3 is that I need to dress and act my age (and also to act like she's her age, i.e., not a baby). I should behave in a manner that is extremely unmemorable, unnoticeable, and inoffensive (dare I say Uncool?). She wants me to be there when she wants me, and not there when she doesn't, like a well-trained servant in an English country manor. Since I'm her mom and not her Jeeves, she's not going to dictate my every move, but I can accommodate her by being as innocuous as I can on her special day. Besides, he's come to see her, not me.

Rule #4

Everyone knows that three's a crowd, but no one is more sensitive to that fact than an adolescent who is with her boyfriend. Rule #4 ("Stay away") reflects that. Regardless of how you see yourself, how fun you think you are, or how close you think your relationship with your daughter is, you are not welcome to join her and her boyfriend when they are alone. Periodically checking up on them to prevent any precocious hanky-panky is fine. You won't be welcome doing that either, but it's your God-given right as a mom.

The odd thing about the practice of hanging out with a daughter when she and her boyfriend are doing something harmless, like watching TV in the family room or playing computer games in an equally public place, is that this noodgy behavior is not limited to either Mrs. Clueless or Mrs. Best Bud. In fact, both types of moms can intrude on their teen's life for their own distinct reasons.

Clueless, for example, will invite herself along because she is either being typically overprotective like some Victorian matriarch who refuses to allow her daughter to spend any time alone with a suitor, or she's just clueless (hence the name) that her daughter is growing up and is at a stage in her life when she needs to start developing age-appropriate relationships with boys. Either way, it's a bummer for her kid, not to mention the boyfriend.

A pernicious form of Best Bud behavior occurs when a woman persists in believing that she is welcome to hang out with her daughter and her daughter's boyfriend. If you find yourself saying, "All the kids love me because I'm so young and hip and up-to-date," then let me paint you a picture: You're fourteen and your own mom is in hip-hugger bells and a halter top sitting with you and your boyfriend as you try to watch

Mod Squad, or worse, enjoy a Rolling Stones album, and you are forced to listen to the lyrics of "Let's Spend the Night Together" while looking directly into your mother's face. You probably greet this thought with a shiver, which is exactly how your daughter is going to react to you plopping down on the sofa with her and her boyfriend to take in a little MTV.

Rules #5 and #6

The final two decrees of my daughter's manifesto (no obscenities) are fairly transparent as to their underlying purpose: "Do not embarrass me by acting like you're on our level." (She found a strange way to express it since I don't regularly walk around the house bellowing like a stevedore, nor do I sit around like I'm at some low-life bar telling off-color jokes.) Quite simply, she's asking me to act like a grown-up.

So what do these six rules mean? I interpret them to mean this: "Don't act like I'm still a little girl" (#1, #2, and #4)—in other words, "don't be Clueless." And "don't act like you're my age (#4, #5, and #6) or that my boyfriend coming over is actually an event for you too" (#3 and #4)—in other words, "don't be a Best Bud." It all adds up to one thing: Be Uncool. Not only does it make your daughter happier, but it's also necessary for her well-being.

Love Means Never Having to Think of Your Mother

A mother who ignores the fact that her adolescent is growing up or who tries to come along for the ride is extremely irritating for a young girl. And when it pertains to boys, it can be humiliating as well as damaging. There is no room for you in her love life except as a chaperone. I don't know about you, but never in my daughter's life do I want my face popping into her mind when she's in a romantic clinch.

Some of you might disagree, saying, "What if it prevents her from doing something I wouldn't approve of?" To that I say: At what point in her life does your face stop popping up? Just because she's married doesn't mean that the association of sex with guilt and mom is automatically going to end. I maintain that by being too intrusive or overprotective, you are compromising one of the vital steps toward her separating and becoming an adult. She is defining herself as her own person— a person who is growing up and starting to have relationships that are a little more grown-up.

Grown-Up *What?!*

Like it or not, kids are going to want to get involved in (calm yourself) more grown-up relationships. It is an essential part of growing up. You know as well as I that it is impossible, not to mention a little weird, for a girl to spend her teens drawing pictures of fairies and unicorns, thinking that sex is yucky, and then suddenly at the age of twenty-two, get married and have children.

It's better to recognize your daughter's awakening sexuality and help her deal with the temptations, challenges, and responsibilities that come with it for as long as you can. From talking to experienced Uncool moms, I've found that the best way to prepare her (and you) is by setting limits and dating rules according to your teen's maturity and responsibility and establishing open communication as early as possible.

Setting Limits

By now I think we all know that the Clueless Mom would set untenable limits akin to "no dating until you're married," and the Best Bud would be so thrilled that her daughter is popular with boys that the thought of responsible parenting would be eclipsed by the excitement of reliving her teen years through her kid's experiences. But what about the Uncool Mom? Like everything else involved with raising a teen, there are no silver bullets. You have to set some general policies and stick with them, but be prepared to hear individual challenges to your authority as well as to be flexible—to consider altering or stretching your policies on a case-by-case basis.

The most common limit that I've heard from other Uncool Moms is that in the early teen years (seventh grade to tenth grade), "a date" as we know it is a multiple-kid affair: going to movies in a group, getting pizza in a group, going to school dances, and so forth. This general policy works very well until, as veteran mom Holly A. says, "about tenth grade, when all hell breaks loose."

The mothers with whom I spoke all cite tenth grade as the time when their daughters started to go on real dates with real boys picking them up in real cars (albeit some with mothers or older siblings driving). Some kids at this time still go out in groups (or stay in: don't think that you can blithely leave them alone in the house now that they're "old enough"—if you come home early, you just might open the door to a teen saturnalia), while some go out on single boy–girl dates.

At this point, apparently you have to rely on everything you've discussed with your daughter about sex as well as her common sense. But it's important not to relinquish your authority completely. Even though your daughter may be sixteen and just a couple of years from being out of your grasp, it's important to continue to have a role in overseeing her safety.

Meet the Parents

Meeting the prospective date is very important, as that's the only time you have to impress upon him the urgency of getting your little sweetheart home in one punctual piece. Coming face-to-face with parents who look like they mean business is going to have more effect on him than if he just stays in the car, honking his horn, bidding your daughter to join him. Anita T. used this opportunity to address some really important issues: "As Jessica and the guy would leave, I would call him over and say just one more thing to him. I would tell him that if he plans on drinking any alcohol that he'd better not plan on driving her home and that I would pick her up."

Julie P. is also not afraid to directly confront her daughter's boyfriend. "Chelsea walks in the house with a huge hickey on her face, so I cornered her boyfriend the next day and I said 'Dan, see that thing on Chelsea's face? I don't want to see anything like that again.' He tries to lie, 'I didn't do it.' So I say, 'Oh, so she has another boyfriend? Someone else is sucking on her face? Look, you're a nice guy, but if you ever put another mark on my daughter, I'm going to kill you.'"

Easier Said than Done

I'm sure the early teen years seem like a cinch to those who are safely past that stage, but for those of us who are still there, we're flying by the seat of our pants. I, for one, am embarking on the uncharted dating territory of my daughter. Having known that this was going to happen sooner or later, I had a policy all ready: She can go places in mixed-sex groups, and she can go out with a boy during the day, but not at night. But it's easy to let your resolve slip when, after getting a surprise phone call from a boy asking her out to a movie at night, she hangs up the phone, throws her arms around you, and is practically delirious with joy. How could I rain on her parade by immediately saying, "Forget it. Not at night."?

So we discussed compromises, such as going to a very early evening or late afternoon show, having me or her dad drive, and going to a nearby, neighborly theater. I'm trying my hardest to be flexible and reasonable, but I know that when she goes off on her date, it's going to make me so nervous I'm going to want to do something screwy, like spy on her.

Admit it, you've wanted to follow your kid the first time she went out alone with friends. It's a powerful impulse that's very difficult to control, but we must. If not, we're in serious danger of acting like the worst example of a parent that I can think of—the sit-com mom.

I spent fifteen years in Hollywood writing and producing TV family sit-coms, some of which (I'm ashamed to say) had episodes of overprotective family members hiding behind potted plants to spy on the young teenage girl on her first date. In my youth, I found this particular sit-com chestnut to be extremely unrealistic and extremely insane. Now that I'm in my early to mid-forties, spying behind a potted plant seems completely plausible. What has happened to me? It's simple—I now have an adolescent daughter.

Alternatives

So, spying is out. What's left? Open communication—and by this I mean not only the frank discussions (*not* lectures) about sex, but also conversations about other aspects of boys. It's important that you be there for her when she wants to gush about her crush, moan about unrequited love, or ask you for some relationship advice.

Giving your teen advice about boys can get you into some very tricky areas that can lead you right to the troubled waters that are home to the Uncool Mom's Scylla and Charybdis: Best Bud-ism and Cluelessness. It's far too easy to slide into either behavior when your daughter actually comes to you for advice.

A Clueless reaction to a boy advice question (assuming that you're not so Clueless that you have passed on to your daughter—subliminally or overtly—the notion that boyfriends are verboten) would be to deny the importance of boys to your child at this age and to trivialize her question or concern with a dismissive response. Saying things like, "You're too young to be in love" or "How could he *not* like you? You're so pretty and nice!" belittles both your daughter and her problems—problems that are very real to her. If you keep it up, your daughter will no longer see you as an understanding adviser whom she can come to and rely on, possibly resulting in her cutting off communication with you at an age when maintaining a connection is so vital.

The Girlfriend Trap

Conditioned perhaps from an early age to giggle and conspire with friends as soon as boy questions are posed to you, you may experience a Pavlovian response—feelings of exhilaration, excessive salivation, and the urge to run to the nearest Girl's Room to whisper and shriek simultaneously with another female. If you find yourself in the grips of such an attack, close your eyes and repeat a settling mantra such as, "I'm over forty," or for difficult cases, "I have cellulite, stretch marks, and crow's feet and haven't played Spin the Bottle since the Carter administration" until it passes.

You have just successfully managed to avoid falling into one of the easiest Best Bud traps you'll ever encounter—giving dating advice to your teen as if you were her girlfriend. Not only does this behavior put you on her level (an Uncool no-no), but also it's quite possible that you'll give her crummy advice—and then have to live through the consequences knowing that it's all your fault.

How It Should Be Done

After a few advice disasters that blew up in my daughter's face, I now give her advice as a mentor, not as a girlfriend. Rather than presenting her with specific directives, I try to help her explore the options available to her, discuss with her the potential consequences (good and bad) of each choice, and then let her carry on to make her own decision. I'm not above providing hypothetical answers to her questions, but it's important that she make her own mistakes, because it is only through those that she will truly learn.

The most important role I have right now is helping her keep perspective about how much this period in her life is going to matter later on. I try to convey to her that in just a few years she won't even remember who Kenny or Drew or Ethan or Jonathan or Kevin or Peter or many of these boys are. She won't have to—I will. I'll remember because these names are being indelibly etched into *my* brain with the almost daily boy stories she relates on our rides home from school. God knows what information it's replacing—I just hope it's trigonometry.

A Separate Life

The gleeful declaration of my daughter's that opens this chapter ("I love it that you hate the boy I like," which, incidentally, isn't true) is on the surface contrary and a little scary. Torturing Mom with an unapproved boyfriend is a favorite form of rebellion among teens, but I wondered if there was something else in what my daughter said—something between the lines—that would give me a clue as to why she said it. Upon further analysis, I realized that she is reveling in having a part of her life—a very important part—completely separate from me. As a matter of fact, the more I don't care for her boy of choice, the more separate she can be from me, which is why she inflated my dispassion into dislike.

Many Uncool Moms have told me: "Even if you detest the boy your daughter brings home, DON'T TELL HER!" So if my sweetie-kins ever brings home Mr. Wrong-in-So-Many-Ways, I'll embrace him and let her use her common sense to figure out he's rotten. As long as she knows that a bad boyfriend is not an effective point of rebellion, I'm sure he will lose his charm—whatever that may be.

Of course, if the boyfriend in question is abusive or involved in dangerous or destructive behavior such as drinking or drugs, all bets are off. Just as I counseled in Chapter 11 regarding dangerous friends, you have the right to intervene to protect your child's safety, which is obviously paramount. It's also wise to seek the advice of a professional before taking drastic actions. They know a lot more about this stuff than we do and may find the right way to put the kibosh on your daughter's relationship with a dangerous scumbag without sending her into his arms.

The Breakup

No matter how useless and redundant our adolescent girls make us feel, they thoroughly need us when they get to this point—the Breakup. It is vital for you to be there for her and to soothe her, not to say, "I told you so." Nothing drives someone away more than that particular reminder.

But if your daughter goes through a breakup at an earlier age (middle school), it's quite possible that her heart isn't broken—her ego is just bruised. At this age, the girl might have been much more into the status of having a boyfriend than in love with that particular boy. Before you conclude that she is devastated, talk to her. It's very easy to make the mistake of assuming that she has the same kind of emotional investment in relationships that older girls tend to make.

When my daughter "got dumped" by her boyfriend Kenny in seventh grade, I was initially worried that she would be crushed. To my surprise, she was just a little angry. I looked over at the cute little stuffed dog that Kenny had given her for Valentine's Day and immediately started feeling a bit apprehensive about its fate.

I said, "What about the stuffed dog? You could give it to your little brother, or you could give it away to charity, or you could decapitate it, hang it—your choice." She replied, "No, it's so cute. I'm not going to take it out on the dog." That's when I understood that it wasn't really about the boy. She wasn't heartbroken—she was just mad that she didn't have a boyfriend anymore. Had she been in high school or college, the cute little dog would have lost its cute little head—cut off and sent back to the creep who dumped her. Back in 1697 when William Congreve decided that Hell has no fury like a woman scorned, he was referring to the girl he dumped in high school, not middle school.

Keeping Perspective

Whether your daughter does pine for a lost love like a torch singer, or whether she just gets aggravated, it's necessary for you both to keep some perspective. She needs to know that she'll get over him, that she is a valuable person with or without a boyfriend, and that life goes on. Make sure your attitude reflects that sentiment. Don't cry when she cries, separate yourself from her personal pain. Be compassionate, be sympathetic, but don't be so empathic that it leads her to believe that the rough patch she's going through is in fact the end of the world.

I've had to think about the "boys" issue for the vast majority of my daughter's life. When she was two and a half and we were checking into a New York City hotel, she sidled up to a wee lad of about four and cooed, "Hi, boy." I'm sure his out-of-town parents were convinced that the prostitution rings in the city had really gone too far this time, but I couldn't care less what they thought—I was too alarmed by my baby's extremely precocious lust. What was I to do with this toddler temptress? If at two and a half she was that seductive, what was she going to be like as a teenager? Mata Hari with braces?

But now that my thumb-sucking siren is thirteen, I am relieved to say that far from being the nymphet I feared she'd become, she actually has a healthy, age-appropriate interest in boys, and enjoys having them just as friends as well. Whew.

I must admit that my husband, the cool head in the family, was key in helping me keep my baby daughter's preternatural interest in the opposite sex in perspective. Never worried, he still thought it important to keep an eye on her and let her know that she is valuable for who she is—she does not need a guy to make her complete. We also established academic achievement as a priority from very early on, which helps to keep her mind on more productive things. Every time she complains about her homework, griping, "When am I ever going to use this math?" I smile to myself knowing that *I'm* the one using it—by keeping her brain too busy to obsess about boys.

The Talk

But perhaps I'm lucky that I know about my daughter's interest. It means that I am always in a position to grab opportunities to chat about sex with her. She is still a little bit precocious in the way she behaves toward boys, yet thoroughly naïve about how boys may read her actions. I regularly discuss with her the realities of getting in over her head with a boy who thinks her signals mean that she's ready and willing. Even though it makes her squirm in her seat, I let her know what moves a date might try on her—holding hands, kissing, petting—and encourage her to figure out what she's comfortable with.

Most important, I remind her of something she learned in preschool: that she is the boss of her own body and that no one can make her do anything she doesn't want to do. She has the right to say no and to express her limit regarding physical affection.

Yes, chatting about sex with your teen is essential. Did you think you could read a chapter about boys and avoid it? Just turn the page—I thought it deserved its own separate little section.

❧ UNCOOL HOT TOPIC ❧
SEX

Say It Ain't So

Don't lie—it just flashed through your mind: "Sex?! Ack!" and you probably had a momentary lapse of oxygen to the brain. Sit down, start breathing slowly and rhythmically into a paper bag, and calm down. When you think you can handle more, read on.

When daughters get to a certain age and we tell them the facts of life, someone should round up the mothers and tell us the facts of life—none of those birds and bees euphemisms, just cold, hard facts about teenagers. The one fact that we foolishly deny is that young humans are going to be sexually attracted to each other, and there is nothing you can do about it. You can sort of hang around on the periphery observing and monitoring teen behavior to prevent your kid from entering into a sexual relationship too early, but at some point, despite your best efforts, it's probably going to happen. It's just a question of when.

It reminds me of an inverse rendition of that strange winter Olympic ice event, curling. Just as you can sweep ice shavings in the way of the puck to slow it down, you can put obstacles in the way of your daughter to slow her down, but eventually both the puck and the girl will get to the finish line.

Love Won't Let Them Wait

One of the best Uncool Moms I spoke to, Tina G., whose daughter Erin is eighteen, says, "In this world today with all the

The NEW MYSTERY DATE GAME For Parents!

➤ *Who will your daughter bring home?*
➤ *What will your reaction be?*
➤ *Who will your daughter fall in love with and want to marry?*

☹ *Loser gets biker boyfriend who daughter will sleep with!*
☺ *Winner gets straight-A boyfriend who daughter will sleep with!*

sexual messages aimed at our youth, it's the rare child who may wait for marriage. When I grew up, you waited, and the rest of the world still had morals. Did I wait until marriage? No. So imagine how hard it is today to convince a child to wait."

She's right. And it's not just the trampy girls who are pursuing an active sex life. Many of these teens are good girls who get good grades and who come from good families—and it was that way when I was a teen too. I remember a group of three girls in our senior year having an unofficial club of nonvirgins. And believe it or not, they weren't the sluts of the school (the sluts started their club sometime in seventh or eighth grade, and by high school the founding members were on maternity leave). In fact, they were all the high achievers: school leaders and A or B+ students destined to attend prestigious colleges.

True, I did go to Sodom and Gomorrah Regional High School, but the point still holds. Sometimes even a well-brought-up and academically successful school leader can succumb to her hormones and/or her romantic ideas about love. And the object of her affection need not be the Danny Zuko's of *Grease*. In my high school the brainy girls had sex with the brainy guys. So don't think you're out of the woods on this one just because your daughter is an honor student who is captain of the swim team and secretary of the Latin Club. You have to realize that when it comes to teenagers and sex, where there's a will, there's a way. As Tina G. says, "Kids are going to have sex, and we are powerless to stop it."

HELP!

At this point you may be panicking—sweating profusely and mumbling repeatedly, "How can I stop this?" Well, you can't. All-girl's school? Sorry. All-girl's schools have the same effect on the human libido as jail does—bottling it up, creating a contents-under-pressure environment so that at the first chance, be it parole (summer camp) or furlough (weekends), the inmates go crazy, releasing their pent-up sexual urges and doing what they can to make up for lost time. As a result, there are plenty of examples of experienced teens coming out of single-sex institutions.

Is the answer a fancy private school attended by the best and the brightest who come from good families that share your values? Ha! At the extremely exclusive and high-ranking private school in my area there is a middle school felatio diva who can perform even while riding a school bus making frequent stops. It'll make for an interesting essay for her application to Yale.

Doin' What Comes Nat'rally

Unlike other teen temptations such as drugs or alcohol, it's important for our children to have positive attitudes about sex for their future happiness and that of their spouses (as well as for ours, vis-à-vis grandchildren). And right there is one of the most difficult aspects about trying to discourage kids from having sex: It's a natural impulse; it's a part of what makes us human. Since there's no genetic imperative to take drugs or abuse alcohol, it's easier to present them as negative and dangerous. It's healthy and natural to want to have sex, but not to want to get drunk or high.

As animals we are programmed to go out and reproduce soon after reaching sexual maturity. As modern humans in our modern society, we consider it important to wait, for practical, moral, and/or religious reasons. The problem that we face as parents is that we're battling a force that is far more powerful than we are: Nature and her pesky little hormones.

No Sex Please, We're Parents

Since for many mothers, trying to stop a daughter from having teen sex is like trying to stop a running bull at Pamplona, the best thing you can do is educate her. Although it may make you queasy to talk to your own child about sex, you have to. Who would you like your daughter to get her birth control information from—you or her idiot friends who will probably tell her that if she jumps up and down right after having sex she won't become pregnant? And then there are other geniuses who may try to give her information, like her eternally horny boyfriend. Mom, like it or not, it's up to you.

The problem is that parents dread the sex conversation so much that when they do broach the topic with their daughters, it's usually because they've found out that the girls are already having sex. For some, that might be too late. Blythe J., a mom with an older daughter, notes, "The most important thing of all, birth control, often seems to be the thing moms do not want to deal with. Almost everyone I know helped her daughter get birth control after a pregnancy scare."

And for those whose daughters don't get the pregnancy scare? Chances are these girls have been lucky so far—making whoopie probably without the benefit of sound advice or reliable information. Many times this is the result of moms, even some who are otherwise Uncool (or even Best Bud), who fall into a Clueless Mom trap of sticking their heads in the sand regarding their daughters and sex. For many women it's too painful to imagine. It's so much easier to deny that their sweet little girls are involved in sexual relationships.

Truly Clueless

Of all the areas of your daughter's life to be clueless about, sex is possibly the worst. Clueless behavior regarding a daughter and boys falls into two categories: virtually locking the girl up à la Rapunzel (which can very easily screw her up psychologically), and dealing with a teen's burgeoning sexuality with denial.

The biggest problem with denial is that the damage that can result goes far beyond the psychological—it can actually endanger her health. Refusing to acknowledge the reality of your child's sexual activity is essentially refusing to acknowledge that your child is at risk for teen pregnancy or sexually transmitted diseases, including AIDS. Would you look the other way, believing that everything's peachy, if you saw a bus barreling down the street your kid is crossing? Then why would anyone delude herself into a false sense of safety when it comes to teen sex?

Perhaps it's some nitwitted notion that if you don't know what's happening, it's not really happening. I've got news for anyone who subscribes to this choice bit of fantasy: If a teenage girl has sex in the forest and no one's there to hear it, not only will she still be having sex, but she'll probably also make a sound.

It may be uncomfortable to talk to your daughter about having sex and birth control, and it's definitely painful to know that she's sexually active, but it's not as painful as taking her to an abortion clinic, an adoption agency, or an infectious disease specialist.

The Brooke Factor

Where does the Best Bud Mom stand on the issue of teen sex? Let's just hope that it isn't along the lines of one of the worst displays of Best Bud-ism in fiction after Susan Sarandon as Brooke Shields's mom in *Pretty Baby*. The depiction I'm referring to is that of Shirley Knight as, yes, Brooke Shields's mom in the movie *Endless Love*, who, upon finding her daughter (Brooke) rutting with her boyfriend on the floor of the family's living room, reacts not with horror, but with a loving and wistful gaze—as if she's watching little Brookie go off to her first day of school. I remember seeing that scene when I was in my early twenties and nearly barfing.

I'm assuming (and maybe I'm just naïve) that this particular scene is not an accurate reflection of how the Best Buds deal with teen sex (although one has to wonder about Brooke Shields's actual mother, who allowed her underage daughter to perform in these movies), but I have heard about equally bizarre practices that are going on in reality in Best Bud homes around the country. Co-ed sleepovers, parties with no adult supervision, parents hiring strippers for a high school party, and carte-blanche prom nights in which the kids don't need to come home or even check in for twenty-four hours.

The Best Bud Form of Denial

It's important to be understanding of a teen's desire to have a sex life, just as it's important to help a daughter get birth control when she decides that it's time, but it's a completely different thing to condone her sexual activity, encourage it, or present her with great opportunities to act on her animal instincts. In a strange way, the Best Buds are probably blinded by their own form of clueless denial—their insane beliefs that their children are adults and that these child-adults are responsible, so they'll be all right.

Children are children, not thinner and better-looking adults, and they are not fictional characters through which parents can relive their wild past or experience a recklessly wanton youth by proxy. I firmly believe that kids want rules. Far from being nasty and unnecessary invasions in their lives, rules, curfews, and limits that curtail their sexual opportunities not only help in keeping them safe and healthy, but also give them a defined sense of how far they have to go to rebel.

The Uncool Tightrope Feat

The Uncool Mom has a very tough job to do, as she has to walk a very fine line. On the one hand, she has to lay down the law and do what she can to keep her daughter from engaging in a physical relationship at too young an age, but on the other hand, she can't demonize sex or shackle the girl to the couch while forcing her to watch an endless loop of *Seventh Heaven* reruns. Likewise, she has to be a source of unconditional assistance and acceptance for her sexually awakening teen, but she can't be the lax and accommodating "do your own thing" dunderhead of a Best Bud Mom either. On top of that, she has to take charge as the firm rule-setter while still providing compassionate acceptance, all without looking like a hypocrite—and have dinner on the table by six-thirty.

From talking to many moms who have found themselves in this predicament, I've come to realize that the key is being nonjudgmental, and the most crucial aspect is remembering that an open line of communication with your daughter is paramount. It's important for a girl to know that if and when she comes to her mother to ask her about birth control—either for curiosity or to procure it—her mother isn't going to scream; ground her; drag her by the hair to a priest, minister, rabbi, deprogrammer, etc.; or have a heart attack. Fear of that kind of reaction from a parent can result in tragedy when a girl, too scared to confide in her parents, disguises her pregnancy and then tries to hide the baby she secretly gives birth to in a closet or bathroom.

Another important advantage to being nonjudgmental is that it helps to keep the issue of sex from becoming a point of rebellion for the teen hell-bent on mutiny. If your daughter thinks that by having sex she will somehow be punishing you, then you might as well give her an engraved invitation and a hotel room. She must understand that early, unprotected sex is only going to hurt herself and that *she* will be left with the consequences—not being grounded or punished, but real-live consequences such as pregnancy or disease. She must always understand that her health and welfare are more important than your opinions or even your values.

A Model Approach

Tina G. is one parent who has done a magnificent job of conveying this sort of nonjudgmental support to her daughter Erin, now eighteen. Tina has been on the case since her daughter was an early adolescent, even though Erin, an honor student and accomplished musician, is hardly the type that would warrant such concern. But Tina knows that appearances can be deceiving, especially when it comes to teen sex, so she's followed a philosophy that centers on prevention—based on knowledge, communication, and nonjudgmental understanding:

When Erin was in eighth grade, Tina talked to her about

all the risks associated with sex—both physical and emotional. But she didn't stop there. When Erin was in tenth grade, Tina had a brainstorm, which in my opinion is something everyone should do with their teens—girls or boys. As Tina relates, "I thought it would be a good idea to have my family doctor, whom Erin adores, speak to her about sex also. I made an appointment, and they privately spoke for forty minutes. He was wonderful with her and showed her graphic pictures of all the sexually transmitted diseases. When they came out of his office, he privately assured me that she is well aware of the risks involved and has a good head on her shoulders. I then told her that even though I really wanted her to wait as long as possible, I wanted her to please tell me when she intends on becoming sexually active. I would rather make sure she is protected than see anything bad happen to her."

It Happens to the Best of Us

The end of this story is not that Erin listened to her mother's request that she wait until adulthood to get into a physical relationship; however, she did listen to the most important things that Tina has been telling her for the last several years. "After going out with a boy for eight months, she said, 'Mom, it's time now to take me to the doctor's for birth control.' I tried to talk her out of it, but it was a losing battle. My heart sank."

Tina took it pretty hard, but she knew that she had to hold up her end of the bargain and help Erin. "It was the hardest and most painful thing for me to do. I wasn't ready for this, but I wanted her to be protected and was thankful that she could talk to me about it. Still, it hurts as her mother, and I wished she could have held out longer."

An Idea Worth Stealing

I'll tell you right now—I'm stealing Tina's method of how to handle a teenager regarding sex. Feel free to follow her example too; Tina won't mind. I've had some very early conversations with my daughter on the topic, but now I know exactly how to proceed. Before she goes to her crazy co-ed camp this summer, I'm sitting her down and discussing some of the more uncomfortable particulars, using Tina as my muse to help me through it.

For most of us, almost all of us, talking frankly about sex and birth control is probably a new parenting skill, but it's one we all must master, no matter how embarrassed, intimidated, or tongue-tied it may make us. It's important enough to put our comfort aside. As mothers, sometimes we have to suffer through some pretty stressful periods for the sake of our children, but we'll deal with it, as we always do. Remember—there was a time when we never thought we'd manage to live through potty training either.

If your daughter seems to have an obsession with sex, or if she is having sex in an indiscriminate, dangerous, or reckless manner, please consult a professional.

Dr. Ava says:

Just as our kids can't imagine us actually "doing it," so we too have a hard time imagining that sweet little body that we used to tuck into bed entwined in the arms of a lover. But by the time your daughter is fourteen or fifteen years old, she is probably on her way to developing a sexual life (remember that the age of sexual initiation is getting younger), and believe it or not—that's good news! It means that you've raised your daughter to be a healthy, loving young woman who is ready to express herself in healthy, loving ways. There are only two problems that loom on the horizon—her choice of partner and the extent of her sexual expression.

Since your daughter needs to make sure her first romantic partners don't remind her of her dear old dad, her earliest choices are likely to be boys from backgrounds very different from yours (therein lies the excitement!). But don't despair—as she learns more about herself and what she needs, her choices usually wind up closer to home. But whatever her choice, remember, *nothing* will cement an unsuitable romance more strongly than your disapproval. So if your daughter's in love with the son of your local hit man (my actual sixth grade boyfriend, by the way), your response should remain politely neutral. (Try, "As long as you're happy, I'm happy, honey.")

Now, what about the extent of her sexual activities? As a mom, I know you're hoping your daughter isn't doing *much* and she isn't doing it *often*. Unfortunately, however, girls are approaching sex these days like President Clinton— it doesn't count (whatever *it* means) if it's not intercourse! So your fourteen-year-old may be engaging in oral or anal sex with her boyfriend while remaining a virgin in her own mind. Further, many teenagers seem to have lost touch with the fact that sex is a physical way to show love; they see sex as an *achievement* not as an *attachment*.

That's why it's so important that your daughter's ideas about sexuality come from you—not from the media or her peers (notably untrustworthy sources). Sex, like all the tough topics we've discussed, is best approached step by step, starting in childhood, when your daughter is two to four (the talk about the differences between boys' and girls' bodies), continuing when she's four to six (the talk about how babies are born), and moving on to your talk to your six- to eight-year-old about sexuality, where your values about trust, commitment, and responsibility need to be included.

By the time your daughter is nine to eleven years old and approaching adolescence, she needs to know about the nature of foreplay, the mechanics of sexual intercourse, the dangers of sexually transmitted diseases, and the sexual practices that will keep her safe. (Forget teaching *abstinence*. It's wishful thinking and a waste of time!)

If you've kept the lines of communication open all along, in the teen years all of this talk will pay off. Your daughter will begin to use her own body to provide her with sexual pleasure, and she'll choose sexual partners who can return her physical affections in a safe and responsible manner. And you, the Uncool Mom, will have raised your girl to become a woman. Congratulations!

15. Uncoolness Now and in the Future

I'm going to put you through so much pain, you're not
going to want me to come home from college.
—Miranda, 15

Who Am I?

While reading through this book, you've probably recognized
yourself as a Mrs. Clueless and a Best Bud as well as an Uncool
Mom. Don't let it confuse you, and don't seek medical attention for it—it's quite normal. Most of us, if not all of us, are a
combination of the various types described here.

Even I, the architect of the Uncool philosophy, lapse into
the very behaviors that I have criticized in these pages. Why? I
refer you to my daughter's quote that opened the book: "You're
hardly a perfect mother." That's right. I'm not perfect. You
don't go to vocational school to learn to be a mother—it's
strictly on-the-job training. As such, you're going to make your
share of whopping mistakes, but you learn from them. The

only difference is that there are no weekends, no vacations, and very few coffee breaks. And the pay sucks.

I see Uncoolness as an ideal—a North Star to navigate by. If you go astray, recognize that you're lost and then reposition yourself. No harm is done if you get back on track.

Ouch!

Remember the story of how my calling my mother "obsolete" practically brought her to tears? How could a thirteen-year-old armed only with a thesaurus inflict such a nasty wound? In my adolescent thrashings, I inadvertently struck at the core of one of her most basic fears—a fear that continually haunts every generation's women as they reach a certain age: the fear of being marginalized by society.

True, we're not going to be sent out on an ice floe or left alone on a forest floor when we reach a particular birthday, but we can be ignored. American culture has its own sort of Logan's Run ethic. If advertisers lose interest in appealing to us, then popular culture can lose interest in us too, and we become extraneous. People who are extraneous become invisible, and then try getting a taxi or a salesperson to help you. After a while, I'll bet the ice floe starts looking pretty good.

Bring It On

Unfortunately, we do not live in the type of society that respects and honors the aged. Perhaps if we did, this fear of marginalization would be meaningless, and the offhanded remark of a rebellious teenager would be insignificant. The youth ideals that were started by the Woodstock generation and then cultivated by those of us who followed is coming back to bite us on the butt. I prefer to approach this situation in the same manner that I would advise my daughter to deal with the popular girls in school: I'm not going to let them push me around.

I have vowed to myself not to deny or fear the natural aging process that is beginning to leave its telltale marks on my body. It's not an easy promise to keep because there aren't too many others who are comfortable abandoning the quest for youth to keep me company. Yep, I'm flying pretty much solo on this one, and I hope I can stick it out because the abject loneliness that occurs during any solitary journey to an uninhabited wilderness can result in the traveler turning back or going mad.

Why do I want to do this? For the sake of my daughter. A teen needs a real grown-up at the controls, not a twenty-something wannabe. (I don't know about you, but I was certainly not wise enough to have been a good mother for a teen when I was in my twenties, so why would I want to go back?) And it helps her sense of security if this grown-up is not buffeted by the whims of a youth-obsessed culture, or by that ever-elusive gold medal called coolness.

Whether it seems so or not, we are role models for our children. The kind of adult your daughter will someday become will be very much influenced by the kind of adult that you are now. It's all a part of Nature's way—we give birth, we bring them up, they leave, we get older, and then they drop their kids off one afternoon right when we are about to go out to see a movie.

Nature's Way

Adolescence is Nature's way of making your kid so unbearable that by the time she's eighteen, you want her out of the house just when she's finding you so unbearable that she can't wait to leave. The parents with the unnaturally peaceful relationship with their teen are the ones whose lives are going to be turned upside down the most when their beloved child leaves.

I guarantee the separation will be easier for both you and your teen if you've got a life outside of mothering. You'll have something to do when the nest is finally empty, and you'll be less likely to see your daughter's rebellion as her sucking the lifeblood out of you. She, on the other hand, will see that your life does not revolve strictly around her, which means that her separation won't crush you. Kids have to feel that the parent they are breaking free from can withstand the blow. Nobody wants to leave her mother if she thinks it's going to crush her.

Obviously, if in the course of her adolescence your daughter ever really needs you, then all the "self" stuff has to take second place. No matter what, you are still a mother, and your child comes first—never doubt that. If she doesn't, maybe you went into the wrong business.

The Devaluation of the Mommy

None of the previous musings about developing a life outside of mothering is meant to demean the role of the mother. In fact, I believe that for me, it's the most important thing I've done in my life. Besides, mothers don't need any more assaults—they've been attacked enough by everyone from Sigmund Freud to Eminem. And today's career-centric society has done a pretty good job of degrading motherhood as well and doesn't need any more help. I would venture to say that the devaluation of motherhood is one of the reasons Best Buds strive to be something other than a mother to their daughters.

I think the problem started when women in the '60s and

'70s rebelled against the traditional view that motherhood was the only thing that a woman could do with her life. But like a lot of people behind ultimately positive social or political steps forward, the hard-core advocates of the Women's Movement went a bit too far, resulting in demonizing those who preferred to be "just a mother."

The Future

So what does the future hold for moms and their daughters? Will the girls who seem to hate their mothers (for no particular reason) in adolescence ever come around? Will we ever make a connection with them? Are they always going to seem so different from us? Every relationship is different, but some women do see little glimmers of a better rapport ahead.

Sharon E., whose relationship with her teen is age-appropriately combative, says, "Tessa knows I adore modern architecture, and of course she hates it, but when she called home while on a school trip to Boston, she told me that she had visited the Le Corbusier building there. She said, 'Mom, you would have really liked it—it's like nothing I've ever seen.' And then she goes on to tell me about the visuals. After I hung up, I just wondered—is this a little pinprick of light? Could she actually be on her way back to me?"

Lassie Come Home

The phenomenon of grown daughters coming back to be friends with their mothers once they have lived a few years as adults reminds me, oddly enough, of a passage from a book I love, *Brideshead Revisited* by Evelyn Waugh. In the novel,

Cordelia Flyte, the youngest daughter of a prominent Anglo-Catholic family quotes from G. K. Chesterton's *Father Brown Stories*, a favorite of her fiercely religious mother:

> *I caught him with an unseen hook and an invisible line*
> *which is long enough to let him wander to the ends of the*
> *world and still to bring him back with a twitch upon the*
> *thread.*

The quote actually refers to God bringing errant Catholics back to the fold, which obviously has nothing to do with being an Uncool Mom, but it has been haunting me ever since I started talking to so many mothers of teens.

The reason is as simple as the image is powerful: Children are connected to their parents by "an unseen hook and an invisible thread," that is, our influence on them—the values we've passed on to them. They can leave us, rebel, and roam as far as they want, but once they are grown and those values click in, they will come to appreciate us and want to return. We don't twitch the thread; our children's better selves do—the adult, independent selves who have the perspective to understand that we're not so bad and may even make a decent friend. The Uncool Mom hopes for this as much as anyone else. She just wants her daughter to leave her as her child, but come back as her friend.

Hope

Here is one final story from an Uncool Mom that I find inspiring. "Mara had a very difficult time during her teen years," relates Linda B. "Two events that happened almost simultaneously—a serious relationship coming to an end and her father moving to Canada—took their toll on her. Her studies began to suffer; she became withdrawn, depressed, and hard to talk to. It was painful to see her go through such a miserable time, and it was made more heart-wrenching by the fact that there was very little I could do to help her.

"I asked an old friend of mine, a psychologist wise about human nature, about what I could do for her. The reply: 'Why don't you just be a refuge to her? You can supply something for her no one else can.' Which was…? 'A lap. Be a lap for her. That's what a mother can provide.' And I have done that.

"About seventeen years after the worst of her teenage years, Mara and I are close. This was the silent wish I maintained through her adolescence: that one day we would get past the shoals and rapids and we would be close, as we were before her adolescence. If she weren't already my daughter, I would want her as my friend.

"She is an artist now, and her first showing of paintings was in New York City. She painted one of a tidal wave, the sun sparkling on the water looming over a sleepy fishing village. This picture is nothing like anything I would have imagined her painting. The wordless source of her art is a mystery to me. I am in awe of it.

"The paintings revealed to me that ultimately you cannot know the private depths of another person, even if you have carried that person in your womb, changed her diapers, seen her first smile, taught her her first words. They also taught me that each person has her own path, her own dark woods to hack through, her own way of coming to understandings which can only be hers.

"In sculptures of kings in the ancient world, the throne the monarch sits upon is actually the body of a woman: The ruler sits upon a lap. As a mother I can only supply a lap for my child, now a grown woman, when she needs one, support her in her search, in her development as a human, but what she does with her essential being is up to her."

My Future

So where am I with my daughter? Now that she's thirteen, I'm back to where I was when she was a tiny infant, searching her face for a little smile—something, anything that will reward me, make it all worthwhile, let me know she loves me. Such a smile would thrill me and fill me with a sense of maternal satisfaction. And then it happens—a lip curls up on one side, then the other. Is it a smile or just gas? Actually, it's something funny she saw on *The Simpsons*. I guess I'm going to have to wait a little longer.

Index